Your First Horse

Your First Horse

A guide to buying and owning

Susan McBane

Stanley Paul

London   Melbourne   Sydney   Auckland   Johannesburg

Stanley Paul & Co Ltd

An imprint of Century Hutchinson Ltd
62–65 Chandos Place, Covent Garden, London WC2N 4NW

Hutchinson Publishing Group (Australia) Pty Ltd
16–22 Church Street, Hawthorn, Melbourne, Victoria 3122

Hutchinson Group (NZ) Ltd
32–34 View Road, PO Box 40–86, Glenfield, Auckland 10

Hutchinson Group (SA) Pty Ltd
PO Box 337, Bergvlei 2012, South Africa

First published 1985
© Gillian Cooper 1985

Phototypeset by Wyvern Typesetting Limited, Bristol
Printed and bound in Great Britain by

British Library Cataloguing in Publication Data
McBane, Susan
Your first horse : a guide to buying and owning.
  1. Horses
  I. Title
  636.1'083   SF285.3
ISBN 0–09–162351–0

Line drawings by Rodney Paull

 Contents

In memory of
ROYAL
my own, much loved, first horse

 Preface

It is said that if you want something badly enough you will very likely get it. To many people who ride weekly at riding schools, or have the odd ride on, or maybe occasionally drive, friends' horses, the dream of having a horse of their own often seems unattainable. They look at other private owners and think how wonderful it must feel to sit on a horse and know that no one can tell you to get off – except possibly the horse himself! Perhaps their dream seems unattainable because they feel it must be horribly expensive to own a horse, because they have nowhere to keep one, or because they do not know enough about the practical side of looking after one.

It is a sad fact that many people cherish such a dream from pony-mad childhood days, when the reasons why they could not have a pony of their own were regularly and firmly instilled into them by reluctant or adamant parents. Those reasons stay with them into adulthood and independence, and their dream remains exactly that – just a dream. But dreams can be turned into goals and ambitions with just a little practical realism; people attain goals and realize ambitions, sometimes long held, every day, and if you go about it the right way for your particular circumstances you too can have a horse or pony of your own – if you want one badly enough. It may take time and it may not be easy, but it *is* possible in most cases. I hope this book will act as encouragement to anyone who has so far only dreamed about owning a horse, and that it will help them firstly to look into the possibilities in a different way – with practical intention rather than wishful thinking – and provide guidelines which will help them achieve their ambition.

Although riding and driving are active sports, they can be enjoyed by almost anyone from small children to the elderly. You don't need the courage of a puissance competitor to enjoy taking part in local shows. You don't even have to have the courage to jump at all if you don't want to. Nor do you need the physical steel of an endurance rider to enjoy hacking about the lanes and bridleways. If you find sitting astride a horse a physical impossibility due, perhaps, to arthritic hips, you can ride side-saddle (to left or right according to your difficulty) and even if you are a man you will certainly not be the only member of your sex to ride side-saddle today!

If you cannot, or do not want to, sit on a horse at all, you may find the sport of driving more fulfilling. Many people turn to driving when they can no longer ride, and find they enjoy it even more. And it does not have to be as expensive as people often think. A leisurely drive with a pony and trap, or a horse and whatever vehicle suits your requirements and means, is much more satisfying and pleasurable than sitting in a car. And competitive driving can be absolutely hair-raising if it's thrills you're after.

If you don't fancy either riding or driving, for whatever reason, you could perhaps follow the example of an acquaintance of mine who just wanted a horse around the place without having to spend too much time on it. She bought a hunter due for retirement with the object of giving it a good home for life, found the horse was bored with no work to do, and developed her own liberty act from a book on the subject. She now gives displays for charity at local shows, and the last I heard was that she had taken in a tiny pony from a rescue charity who is also joining the act!

In short, there are countless ways in which you can enjoy having a horse of your own. Your circumstances – physical, domestic and financial – will determine how far you can go and what sports you can take part in, but even on an 'ordinary' wage it should be possible to buy, keep and enjoy a horse of your own.

If you are a parent thinking of buying a pony for your child, you may well feel overfaced by the apparent difficulties, particularly if you yourself are not 'horsey'. However, many of today's top equestrian stars in the different disciplines are the children of parents who knew nothing about horses or ponies. I stress the word 'knew' rather than 'know' as, once their child gets the bug, parents often find themselves forced into reading up about ponies and learning as much as possible about them, in order to help their offspring enjoy the sport in safety. Also, the pony

8

becomes very much a part of the family, once purchased, needing care and attention just as much as the family dog.

In cases where parents really do not feel able to absorb such knowledge, it is still possible for them to indulge their child and buy him or her a pony *provided* it is kept at a reputable stable where knowledgeable advice, care and supervision, not to mention instruction, are available. It would be foolish, dangerous for the child, and probably cruel to the pony for unknowledgeable parents to allow an almost as unknowledgeable (if frantically enthusiastic) child to keep a pony at home or in rented accommodation with no expert help or supervision.

The advice in this book on guideline standards of competence, on where to get expert help and on suitable livery services will be of as much help to parents wanting a pony for their child as to purchasers buying an animal for themselves. One of the secrets of overcoming lack of knowledge and experience is knowing where to acquire it, if only in the form of expert counselling, and this book can certainly help in that direction.

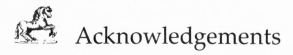 # Acknowledgements

For permission to reproduce photographs included in this book, the publishers and author would like to thank Carol Gilson, *Horse and Rider*, Kit Houghton, E. A. Janes, Bob Langrish, and Graham Trott.

The author would like to express her appreciation of the help given with this book by Gillian McCarthy, BSc Hons, Northwood Riding Centre, Gorsey Lane, Bold, Widnes, Cheshire, and Margot Tiffany BHSI.

1. The Horse for You

People's taste in horses is as personal as their taste in friends. If you have been riding regularly, probably for some years, at a riding school, you will have come into contact with a wide variety of animals. Friends' horses and ponies, too, add to your experience and you may have a good idea of the kind of horse you want and whether you want to ride or drive.

Many experienced and professional horsepeople feel that the only horse worth considering is one which is a Thoroughbred or very nearly so and, although it may be tempting to go for a glamorous and impressive breed such as this (and by no means all Thoroughbreds are hot-headed lunatics), unless you are yourself experienced and competent it may be wiser to plump for something a little more down to earth for your first horse.

You need a horse who feels right under you – a comfortable height and neither too wide nor too narrow for you to sit easily and relaxedly. He (or she) needs a temperament which complements your own. If you are a calm, confident person you could have a beneficial effect on a horse which is lively and outgoing. On the other hand, if you are a little nervous or highly strung, the last thing you need is a horse with a similar temperament; go for a sensible, tolerant animal who will not be upset by any neurotic 'vibes' you may give out!

Sex can make a difference, too. Some people naturally lean towards one sex whereas others do not mind either way. For your first horse I should recommend, however, that you do not buy a stallion (an uncastrated male, sometimes called an entire) because they do need competent, sympathetic handling. If your horse leads a normal life he is bound to meet up with other

13

animals, and if you come across a mare in season your stallion could very well become quite uncontrollable, or at the very least a considerable nuisance, unless he can be relied upon to behave impeccably for you.

Mares, too, being undoctored – it is very unusual to find a mare who has been sterilized – can sometimes be unpredictable and moody when in season, which they will be every three weeks. So unless you particularly want a mare or can put up with mare-ish behaviour you should choose a gelding – a castrated male. Mares can cost more than a gelding of similar quality, as the vendor always maintains that you can use her for breeding and so make a profit out of her. In practice, it is difficult to make a profit out of a single mare (or even an entire herd) unless she is of very good quality (expensive!) and sent to high-class stallions (also expensive!). Most breeders will tell you that when the stud fees and keep/veterinary costs have been totted up over the years, by the time the youngster is of a suitable age to sell for breaking in, you will be lucky to break even, let alone make a profit.

Whatever their temperament, nobody likes the type of horse commonly called a 'plug'. These are horses or ponies which plod along, bored with life, possibly sullen in nature, and who require herculean efforts on the part of their riders to progress into a few steps of trot. There is a lot of difference between a plug and a calm, sensible horse who is willing to go, to stop (just as important!), to turn, jump if you want to and generally join in and enjoy your company. Such paragons *do* exist and, for your first time, it would be well worth the effort of finding one.

Perhaps most important of all, you must like each other. Meeting a horse for the first time is just like meeting a person or a dog. You can feel an instant rapport or dislike, or you might take the whole of your first meeting to find out whether you like each other or not. Obviously, if you do not like each other you will never have much fun, so there is no point in your being together.

How Good Are You?

Your own experience will also dictate what kind of horse you should buy. What do we mean by a 'competent rider' or a 'novice rider'? It is a useful rule of thumb to be guided by the British Horse Society examinations designed for BHS members, for members of riding clubs affiliated to the BHS and for those wishing to enter the horse world as a profession. The fact that someone has been riding for many years does not automatically mean he or she is a competent rider – experienced, yes, but not necessarily good. The instruction and education they have received, and the way they have responded to it, will give a much better idea. This book is intended mainly for people, adults or children, who have been attending a good riding school (one approved by either or both of the British Horse Society and the Association of British Riding Schools, about which more later), have received sound instruction and are reasonably capable.

If you have reached British Horse Society Stage II standard (Grade II for riding clubs, or 'C' Test standard if you are in the Pony Club), you will be able to ride and handle, and care for under supervision, a well-mannered animal who is willing and obedient in walk, trot and canter, be able to perform simple movements such as turns and circles, lead the animal in hand and jump little fences up to about 2 feet, probably smaller. You will be able to talk about and demonstrate at a basic level aspects of horse care including feeding, grooming, foot care, bedding and exercise, tack and equipment and have a basic knowledge of minor ailments. Such a person should be capable of owning and enjoying a quiet, obedient animal, but would not know enough to care for it without supervision.

The Stage III, Grade III and 'B' Test standards cover people who show a reasonably secure, balanced seat in the saddle and can jump show jumps or cross-country fences up to about 2 feet 9 inches in height. They are expected to be able to handle and ride well-mannered animals with a degree of aplomb, but are not expected to cope with difficult animals. A candidate who reaches this standard must have sufficient knowledge of all aspects of basic horse care to be able to look after properly for a fortnight a fit, corn-fed animal. In short, you should be capable of looking after your own horse unsupervised, but should know when situations arise which you are not competent to handle, and whom to call on in such cases.

If you have never considered what standard you are, now is the time to ask your instructor at your riding school. There is no need to take the examinations if you don't want to, but you need an honest opinion of whether or not you are truly competent enough to have a horse of your own.

I should never recommend an utter novice to buy a horse of their own unless expert help and supervision are constantly available. Riding can be a dangerous activity; insurance companies certainly regard it as a 'risk' sport, and in the interests of your own safety and that of your horse or pony and the world at large, you should be reasonably knowledgeable and capable before embarking on horse ownership. On the other hand, you do not need to be brilliantly competent to enjoy yourself in safety, provided your horse is suitable for you and an asset rather than a liability.

Those wanting to drive rather than ride are in a more difficult position as there is no recognized network or approval scheme for horse-driving schools. There are several establishments dotted about the country (although nothing like so many as riding schools) and you may be able to get the name and address of a reputable school or freelance instructor/adviser from one of the driving organizations listed in Appendix A. The school proprietor will be able to give you a good idea of your competence. If you have had no formal instruction but have perhaps been driving friends' animals, it would be worthwhile attending a proper course during your holidays to acquire a grounding in the discipline.

People who have been riding or driving other people's animals, whether those of friends or those at a school, can often get quite good in the saddle or on the box seat but lack the most rudimentary knowledge of how to look after a horse. For this reason, Chapter 8 of this book contains details of the basics of horse and pony care and management. I also recommend you to take a course in practical horse care (stable management) before you set about buying your horse, because once you realize just what is involved in looking after a horse adequately you may feel it is all too daunting and put off the big day until you have somehow gained more experience in this very important aspect of horse ownership. Black, freezing mornings, rain dripping down your neck, blue fingers and toes, mud in your boots and backache from all the bending and lifting, not to mention the tying responsibilities if you are doing the horse yourself, have caused many a would-be owner to forego ownership or at least keep the horse at livery – not so satisfying, but much more convenient.

Many establishments run week-long courses in stable management or have lectures and practical sessions, say, one evening a week. These courses are most useful and will be a big help if stable management is not your strong point. Even if you are going to keep your horse at livery so that he will be cared for by someone else, he is *your* horse and, in law, he is your responsibility whether you look after him yourself or not. Therefore it is
16

imperative to know whether he is being cared for properly. However, you will doubtless want to know that your horse is happy and well anyway, because you will probably come to care a great deal for him, so the more knowledge you acquire yourself, the better you will be able to look after him – or ensure that someone else does the job properly.

Money!

It is unfortunately true that horses are expensive animals both to buy and keep. It costs less to keep a horse at home and do him yourself because you have no rent or labour charges. A slightly more expensive method is to keep the horse in rented accommodation but still look after him yourself; next up the line is to keep him at part or full livery (i.e. in a commercial yard or riding school, paying for his board and lodging and also labour charges for the staff to look after him); and the most expensive way is to employ your own groom.

At the time of writing (1985), if you are keeping your horse at home and looking after him yourself you must be able to allocate £20 a week averaged out over the year to account for feed, bedding, shoeing and veterinary expenses – and this will not account for any extra being put aside for transport expenses, show entries, major items of tack and equipment or veterinary requisites, insurance fees, club or society memberships or your own clothing.

At the other end of the scale, if you are keeping the animal at full livery you can expect to pay, for a horse, from £30 to £45 a week depending on the area. This should account for stabling, grazing, exercising, bedding, feeding and general care such as grooming, nursing when sick etc. It will not cover shoeing (this currently costs from £10 to £20 for a full set of new shoes which will probably be needed every six weeks, especially if your horse goes on hard roads), veterinary expenses or a contingency for buying tack, rugs and grooming kit replacements and so on. These costs will be less for a pony.

The initial cost of the animal itself can range from about £500 for a fair, all-round family animal to about £1,000 for a youngish but mature horse capable of bringing home a rosette at local shows and events. If you get bitten by the competition bug you can, of course, pay considerably more than this. At the top end of the scale, international showjumpers regularly fetch five-figure sums and top racehorses not uncommonly fetch millions nowadays – and untried at that! So you see, you can pay almost anything for a horse; it all depends on what you want.

The horse's equipment can easily cost as much as the animal himself. A good, new, general-purpose saddle can cost about £300 and a bridle with the bit (always extra) £50, or less. A set of driving harness can cost anything from a few hundred (for exercise harness – and sets of cheaper, non-leather but quite adequate equipment are available) to a few thousand for a top-quality, show-standard leather set. Winter rugs are very varied, ranging from very roughly £25 to £50 depending on the type and size you want. You will need more than one, for laundering purposes. If the horse is going to be clipped, you will also need blankets, and there are extraneous items to consider such as bandages, boots, buckets, a headcollar, grooming kit and first aid supplies.

All these things need weighing up carefully before a horse or pony is purchased. Horse ownership is not, indeed, a cheap pastime, but I repeat what I said in the Preface – it should be possible, with prudence and common sense, even for people with a moderate income to be able to buy and keep an animal.

The price of the horse or pony himself is governed by breeding, age, capabilities (the more he can do, the more he might cost) and health. 'Mongrel' (not a term normally applied to horses, but very descriptive) horses tend to cost less than purebreds or good crossbreds with registration papers, just as pedigree dogs cost more than Heinz types. A horse's price tends to appreciate up to about seven or eight years of age, from roughly nine to twelve it levels off (these are generally regarded as a horse's prime years) and from twelve onwards the price tends to fall. However, there is nothing wrong with getting an older horse. Many of fifteen and over have several useful years left, particularly if your work is not particularly strenuous. They are worldly-wise and often make good 'nannies' to their first-time owners. Some, though, do get crafty with age, not to mention wilful, and end up being boss – never a good situation! Much depends on the individual animal's temperament, character and health.

Very few horses are in perfect health (and very few humans, come to that), but this does not matter if your work is not going to make demands with which they cannot cope. A slight, but insignificant, health defect can knock a considerable chunk off the price of a horse no longer able to do his original, demanding job. For example, if you want a horse to carry you quietly around the lanes and bridlepaths with the odd canter, it will not matter if the horse's wind (respiration) is not as good as it could be, because he will not be put under much stress. Similarly, a heart murmur need not cause you to reject him if you are not going to be doing fast work with a lot of galloping and jumping. Your veterinary surgeon, who should examine the horse before purchase, will advise you fully on the animal's state of health, so you must be honest about what you intend to do with the horse. Then the vet can tell you whether, in his or her professional opinion, the horse's health (or state of soundness) will enable him to do that job safely without detriment or danger to himself or you.

Time Available

Horses not only cost money, they take up time, particularly if you are looking after them partially or entirely yourself. They need *daily* attention all year round, and not just once a day. A stabled horse who needs mucking out, bedding down, feeding, grooming and (most time-consuming of all) exercising can easily take up three or four hours a day, depending on the amount of work he's doing – and it's as well to remember that a healthy horse should have a good two hours' exercise a day, and/or be turned out in a field for at least that long, if he is to remain happy in mind and healthy in body.

If you are caring for him yourself, you will have to consider your time schedule in detail. If you have a job with fixed hours, the horse will have to be fitted in around it, which will mean early mornings, late evenings and maybe lunchtime dashes, too. Family commitments also come into it; if your family all want to be involved with the horse you could find your workload considerably lightened, but if they don't, it could be all down to you and you may still have domestic responsibilities, too. Hopefully, your family will at least cooperate on the domestic front, maybe with a little subtle re-education!

A child's pony kept out and used only at weekends in winter will take the minimum time, say half an hour morning and night checking over, basic grooming, maybe feeding and checking of field and shelter and removal of droppings in the latter.

Please understand that this care must be administered without fail every day of the year. Horses and ponies are not toys or machines which can be put away out of sight and mind when they are not being used. If you cannot provide at least twice-daily 'servicing' yourself or within the family, alternative arrangements will have to be made. You can either get paid help or you can keep the animal at livery (see Chapter 3). This will cost more, but, as ever, time is money. If you do not have the time available yourself to care properly for a horse or pony, you will have to buy someone else's time and services.

Sharing

One method of ownership which can help alleviate time and money problems is sharing a horse or pony with someone else. It seems to be fairly common these days for two friends to buy a horse together, share his keep costs and work out a mutually acceptable rota of who has the use of him and when. The success of such an arrangement obviously depends on your relationship with your partner. If you can find someone with whom you can build up a friendship, who is flexible and reasonable over your use of the horse and who wants the same kind of animal as you do, you could be onto a winning arrangement.

Unfortunately, such arrangements can go sour very quickly, particularly if you do not actually have a half share of the horse. For instance, if you come across someone who already has an animal but is finding the time and costs too much, you could go halves with the expenses and work, but find yourself out in the cold when it comes to major decisions such as going to an important show. 'After all,' your partner might point out, 'he is *my* horse.' Also, if you get really fond of the horse and your partner decides to sell him, you could be in for a lot of heartbreak if you cannot take him over yourself.

If you do want to try a horseshare arrangement, I would advise you to pick your partner and the horse very carefully. Having done that, do get an agreement drawn up in writing, mutually agreed and signed by both parties, which covers exact costs to be paid by both of you (with annual reviews), the time each of you is entitled to use him and, in the case of a jointly owned horse, that each has the option to purchase him should the other partner decide to sell his or her share.

Talk about your arrangement to a reputable insurance company, too (more information in Chapter 4), to sort out a policy which covers both of you for third party liability (free, incidentally, to British Horse Society members), personal accidents, injury to or death of the horse. Some companies refuse to pay out

20

for any item not involving the legal owner of the horse, and, with respect to them, insurance companies are as ingenious as tiny ponies at wangling their way out of 'unacceptable situations' – ponies get out of fields, and insurance companies get out of paying if they can possibly find a loophole. So talk it over very carefully, get everything in writing, and also discuss the matter with a solicitor when you have the final proposed policy.

Even with a good agreement, share arrangements are no use at all if you are in partnership with someone you can't talk to or reason with, and in many people's experience sharing a horse is something they would not wish to repeat. You may be lucky, but the arrangement must be gone into with much forethought and care.

Accommodation

The question of where you are going to keep the horse may not be the least of your problems. The first thing to consider is what sort of accommodation the animal needs. There are varying opinions as to the best method of keeping a horse and these are discussed in Chapter 2.

Some people keep their animals stabled all the time and never turn them loose in a field; others keep them out all the time and never stable them; while yet others use a combination of both methods. I feel, to cater for all eventualities, that you should have both a stable and grazing area available, but this is not the end of the matter.

Most horses need the company of another of their own kind. Some do live solitary lives and survive adequately, but horses are by nature herd animals and most of them feel unhappy and insecure without the company of other horses. Those kept almost entirely alone often form attachments to other animals such as the stable cat, the family's pet dog or even goats, sheep and hens. It is common for racehorses, who have other horses around but are not turned loose with them while in training, to form friendships of this kind with other species.

So you will almost certainly have to provide your horse or pony with equine company if he is to be truly happy. If you are thinking of keeping your horse at home, this could mean you may have to find the means and accommodation for two animals, not one; alternatively, perhaps you could stable your horse at home, but arrange daily grazing nearby in the company of other horses.

21

You may well be able to provide company for your horse by having a horse-owning friend keep their animal with you. This often works well from the point of view of labour, too, as you can take it in turns to do the horses, as your circumstances demand. One of the biggest drawbacks to being solely responsible for the care of animals is that when you are too ill to cope they are bound to suffer to some extent, so a friend and his or her horse on the premises can work well for both of you.

If you do not want this arrangement, company could be provided by means of 'adopting' a small pony from an equine rescue charity, provided you meet their requirements as regards standard of knowledge, care and accommodation. (Incidentally, if you do *not* meet those, quite reasonable, standards, you should be thinking twice about your own suitability to have sole charge of your horse or pony.) This sort of arrangement can be suitable for those able to pay for their animals' keep but not able to find the capital for purchase.

A stable has to be a fairly roomy building (see Chapter 3) and strongly built because horses, and even small ponies, are strong animals quite capable of demolishing (gradually or all at once) a flimsy building, particularly if they are in it too long and boredom sets in. A converted poultry hut or asbestos garage will not do! Turn-out facilities are a great advantage and can range from a little area just big enough for the horse to get up a short canter and kick up his heels to several acres of good grazing land. If you cannot provide a turning-out area, can you be sure you can give your horse at least two hours' exercise every day (preferably in two stints) to compensate for the lack of freedom and provide him with the physical activity he must have to keep him healthy and happy?

It is true that many horses, particularly military and police horses, are kept for years without ever being turned out, and although this may not be ideal, such horses do have considerable and regular work – much more than the average private owner gives his or her animals. For the rest of us, who may only be able to give intermittent or restricted exercise, I do feel that somewhere to turn out the horse, if only when other exercise cannot be given, is essential.

In addition to stabling and grazing, you will need somewhere to store your feed, tack and other equipment, not least of which will be your vehicle if you wish to drive. Hay and bedding are bulky and can take up a lot of storage space. An average-sized family garage will only store enough hay and straw for one horse for a very few months. A 15.3 hands high horse will eat roughly two to three bales of hay a week and use up about the same amount of straw. Then you will need somewhere to store your concentrate food (nuts, grain etc.) in bins, your grooming kit, rugs, saddle, bridle, harness, mucking out tools – and where will your muck heap be?

If you cannot provide suitable facilities at home you will have to find them elsewhere. Then you have to consider whether it is reasonably convenient for you to visit the horse. This becomes especially important if you are looking after him yourself. An hour's journeying time per day is quite a chunk, and you will have to visit at least twice a day unless someone else is sharing the chores.

If you are paying for livery, you could end up only being able to see your horse at weekends if the horse is a considerable distance from your home and you have other commitments such as work during the day. Many owners are in this position, in fact, but you have to consider whether it is what *you* want. If you want to see the horse most days and ride before or after school or work at appropriate times of year, you will have to find somewhere closer to home, which may not be easy. From my own experience, and from talking to other people, I have found that being unable to find or provide suitable accommodation for a horse or pony is the major reason why most would-be owners do not have one, not lack of money, so this is a very important hurdle to overcome before even thinking of actually looking after a horse.

Of course, if you are very keen, you may well arrange your life so that you live in an area conducive to horse keeping. This means jobs, schools and family/friend contacts have to be considered carefully, but the fact remains that many owners live and work where they do simply because their horses are a big part of their lives and the area they have chosen enables them to live the life they want to, that is with horses in the family.

Breeds and Types

There is a suitable breed or type of horse or pony for everyone. You will probably have some idea of the kind you want. This book is meant to be a general guide on the most important aspects of acquiring your first horse or pony. It is not intended as a specific manual on horse management, on anatomy, conformation and physiology, on equitation or veterinary matters.

However, throughout the book an effort is made to guide the reader to authoritative, more detailed sources of practical help or reading matter.

This section on breeds and types does not, therefore, deal with specific points of conformation or laid-down breed standards. Two excellent books on 'make and shape' are recommended in Appendix B, Recommended Books, while Appendix A, Organizations and Societies, gives addresses of breed societies and similar bodies who can supply you with detailed descriptions and requirements for their particular breed or type. Also, as this is your *first* horse, I advise you most strongly to engage a professional to assess, and maybe find, an animal for you. Such an adviser (see Chapter 4) will have a good knowledge of the important matter of conformation in relation to the work the horse will be able to do, and the vet you engage to check the horse for health and soundness will give a second opinion on these two points.

Therefore, I hope you will take this section for what it is – a general guide to the type of animals available so that you can consider what is available and discuss matters with your adviser.

Thoroughbred

Most competent and experienced horsemen regard the Thoroughbred as the riding horse par excellence. A good one is the essence of refinement and quality – fine-skinned, with a silky coat and hair, responsive, courageous, alert, fast and intelligent – everything you could want in a riding horse. Against them, it can be said many are hot-headed, easily upset, nervous, over-sensitive physically and not the easiest horses to look after.

The true picture is probably somewhere in between. Because Thoroughbreds were bred initially from predominantly oriental horses native to hot climates, they are certainly not the best candidates for wintering out in Britain. They do feel the cold and damp more than some other types of horse, so if you are thinking of keeping your horse outdoors all year round, a Thoroughbred would not be your best choice.

As to temperament, I have known many very placid Thoroughbreds, and it must be remembered that the way a horse behaves can depend largely on how he has been schooled and how he is handled and ridden or driven. In general, however, Thoroughbred horses demand excellent management and riding; if you can provide these essentials you may be happy with a Thoroughbred for your first horse. If not, but you want Thoroughbred blood, pick a horse which is part-TB only. Many of Britain's top show-jumpers and event horses are seven-eighths TB, the remaining eighth being anything from native British pony to Clydesdale. This dash of 'common' or pony blood gives that little bit of extra hardiness and common sense frequently lacking in pure Thoroughbreds. Three-quarter Thoroughbreds are often excellent crosses, with quality and substance combined. Halfbreds, obviously, are even more down to earth, but can still be good-looking, active horses ideal for a first-time owner.

Because the Thoroughbred is a relatively 'young' breed, barely 250 years old, there is still a wide range of types. Some individuals plainly show their cold-blooded, heavy ancestry while others look very much like their Arabian founding fathers. Height, too, ranges widely, with a few specimens in the 14–15 hands range, some 17 hands and over, but most ranging within the 16 hands-plus area.

Arab

The Arab is definitely a hot-blooded breed. This does not mean that its body temperature is any higher than that of other breeds, but that it is a purely oriental horse evolved in hot climates. It is thin-skinned, grows a short coat (even its winter coat is fine and silky) and is the foundation breed for the Thoroughbred. It is certainly one of the oldest and purest breeds in the world, being several thousand years old, and its true origins have never been proved. There are many theories, but the most likely is that it originated in the form we would recognize today (that proud head and tail carriage, flaring nostrils and springy step) in ancient Mesopotamia and only appeared in Arabia in any numbers in the seventh century AD when the astute prophet Mohammed realized the value of such horses for his military campaigning.

I feel Arab horses are sadly misunderstood in many areas of the horse world. In my experience this is mainly because they do not suffer fools gladly: despite the fact that when wisely handled they are faithful, generous, tractable and sweet-natured, in incompetent, rough or weak hands they quickly gain the upper hand, stand up for themselves and answer back. This has given them the reputation, among those who do not understand the breed, of being uncooperative, stubborn, wilful and even stupid. In fact, Arab horses are intelligent (and need intelligent owners), and have great stamina and considerable speed, razor-sharp reactions and an inbred ability to stop on a sixpence. They are not

25

beginners' horses, but if you are experienced, sensitive and have a feel for this breed, you will probably be content with no other.

Anglo-Arab
An excellent cross between the two breeds discussed so far is the Anglo-Arab. To qualify for this description, and registration as such with the Arab Horse Society of Great Britain, an animal must have at least 25 per cent Arab blood. Whereas Arabs tend to be smallish – few are over 15.2 hands high, if that – Anglo-Arabs often have the height of the Thoroughbred with the extra fire and more sensible temperament of the Arab; a good specimen will combine the qualities of both breeds, both physical and mental.

Thoroughbred and Arab crosses
Both the Thoroughbred and, especially, the Arab have been used extensively to cross with heavier horse and pony breeds; while this often results in greater refinement and quality, enthusiasts for some of the other breeds have said that it causes loss of hardiness (meaning resistance to our winter climate), which it doubtless does. The Welsh ponies of Sections A and B (children's riding ponies) have a great deal of Arab blood in them yet retain their pony character and constitution. Experiments in the past to combine Arab blood with other breeds have been less successful and have been stopped in time to prevent over-saturation with 'foreign' blood.

It is important to note, however, that many truly excellent horses and ponies are crosses between Thoroughbreds and/or Arabs and/or native or 'mongrel' animals and, in general, Thoroughbreds and Arabs cross well with almost any breed if the individuals are selected wisely. Particularly if you are looking for a horse rather than a pony, you will almost certainly be shown one with some Thoroughbred or, less commonly, Arab blood.

Irish Draught
One breed of horse which is being promoted as a solid, sensible all-rounder with a good temperament, good conformation, free action and a willingness to please is the Irish Draught. This breed was threatened with extinction not so long ago, but is now well on the way to being widely accepted again. Although used by Irish farming families to work on the farm, take produce to market and provide a day's hunting, and in Ireland's towns and cities for haulage, it is definitely not a heavy, sluggish animal: good specimens show substance and energy plus quality and a

certain refinement; many have considerable jumping ability. In the past, they were regularly crossed with Thoroughbreds to produce hunters with a little more quality and speed than the pure-bred Irish Draught. The next cross on (three-quarters TB × one-quarter ID) was regarded by many as the perfect hunter in any type of hunting country, with much of the Thoroughbred's ability and that dash of common sense shown by native-breds of Great Britain and Ireland. The purebred would certainly make a good first horse and it is not difficult to find in Britain.

Cleveland Bay
This breed is Yorkshire through and through, having the individuality and independence of its native breeders. Particularly when crossed with Thoroughbreds, they make superb carriage horses and, purebred, make good middle- to heavyweight hunters, depending on the individual. Like the Irish Draught, they nearly became a thing of the past earlier this century, but are now well established again. Perhaps their enthusiasts will forgive me if I say that, due to a tendency in many individuals to be a little wilful and independent, Cleveland Bays do not make ideal first horses.

Cob, hunter and hack
The cob is generally a type of horse rather than a breed, as are the hunter and the hack. These terms cause a good deal of confusion among newcomers to the horse world. 'Cob' initially means nothing to them, 'hunter' means any animal which hunts, and 'hack' sounds as though the animal in question is on its last legs! I'll try to be a little more helpful and attempt the difficult task of defining these terms.

An animal of cob type is generally medium-sized (no higher than 15.2 hands). It is a stocky animal with shortish legs, strong quarters in particular, a strong but elegant neck and a head which should not be coarse-looking. As with any horse or pony, it should have a pleasant facial expression and, as a type, cobs often have patient, quiet temperaments. A good specimen would make an ideal first horse for someone wishing for a family friend able to perform a bit and, if necessary, able to live out all year round given reasonable facilities.

The hunter type, as defined by showring requirements, falls into one of three categories, mainly lightweight, middleweight and heavyweight, the divisions decided by the weight the horse is felt able to carry.

27

It may be confusing to be told that hunters vary in size and body weight according to the type of quarry to be hunted (e.g. foxhunters invariably prefer a Thoroughbred type of animal able to gallop on over a predominantly fast grass country, whereas harrier followers, hunting hares, often have heavier, slower animals), the weight of the rider and the type of country. A 'trappy' country, with awkward turns, tricky obstacles and a lot of ploughland requires a nippier, handier but slower animal. The best way to get your eye in for type is to go to as many good regional and county shows as you can, and study the type of the animals entered in the different classes.

A physical description of a good hunter type might be that he has a body (trunk) of generous proportions to allow plenty of room for heart and lungs, and quarters of significant musculature and build to propel that body over the countryside during a long day. His shoulders must be 'well laid back' or 'well-sloped' (a term explained in Chapter 6) and be long enough from nose to back to give the rider in the saddle the feeling that he really does have something in front of him. This latter expression is often termed 'length of rein' and incorporates the length of the neck, which must be long enough to help the horse balance himself in difficult terrain or over awkward obstacles. The head should not be big and coarse, but plainness is often found in hunter types. It is no disadvantage even in the showring, provided it is combined with an honest expression and that hard-to-define asset, quality.

In showring parlance, the hack is the epitome of everything a horse ridden for pleasure, as opposed to pure sport, should be; the type is divided into the Small Hack (not over 15.1 hands high) and the Large Hack (not over 15.3 hands high). Ladies' hacks of any height are usually ridden side-saddle. The word 'hack' is peculiarly British, and is an old word used to define an animal which is definitely a quality riding horse. Hacks, in the heyday of the horse when the terminology was formulated, were not expected to hunt, and such animals were used as 'covert hacks' (meant to carry owners and grooms to and at coverts in the hunting field, but not to follow hounds) and 'park hacks', very elegant, refined animals on whom one was proud to be seen riding in the park. These animals were often highly trained in what is now called dressage, and such movements as half-pass and full-pass plus superb collected paces enabling the rider to ride with one hand on the lightest of contacts (as occasionally seen in high-class showrings now) were commonplace. The most

28

beautiful animals normally found jobs as ladies' hacks and, even today, these are the ones who tend to win hack classes in the showring. Any show animal should have impeccable manners, but this applies particularly to hacks.

Looking at old photos of hacks, one can see that, compared with some of today's animals, the type is not as common as it was before the Second World War, when a definitely recognizable type existed. Today, many hack classes are filled with animals which lack sufficient quality and refinement, and that magnetic 'presence' possessed by life's winners, human and equine, and which should be regarded as essential in a show hack.

In practical terms, a hack is any animal suitable for riding. Many racehorses retire to become the trainer's hack on whom he accompanies his string to the gallops and from whose back he observes the morning's work, and many hunters (just to confuse you further) retire to become hacks for people wanting a horse to take them on pleasant rides round the countryside. (Such rides are also called hacks! And riding out like this is called hacking.)

If you want something a little smaller than a horse (into which category fall hunters and hacks) an animal of cob type would possibly suit you well. There is no 'legal' height limit between ponies, cobs and horses – they each have their own character, and, although for general purposes any animal over, say, 14.3 hands can be regarded as a horse and any under that height as a pony, an animal of 15.1 hands of 'chunky' build may well be called a cob, whereas a Thoroughbred of the same height would certainly not be! I do not mean to confuse you, and assure you that these nuances of description will become second nature to you if you take a little trouble to study them at good shows.

You might also consider the larger of Britain's native breeds, most of which prove to be real family all-rounders suitable for adults and children alike.

Welsh ponies
Officially, there are four sections or types of Welsh breeds. The Section A or Welsh Mountain Pony is not more than 12.2 hands high officially, although they do come larger, so is only suitable for small children.

The Section B or Pony of Riding Type is not more than 13.2 hands, and, despite being accused, with some justification, by purists of being an 'invented' breed because it contains a good deal of non-Welsh blood, it is now most popular as a truly excellent children's riding pony – although it is a boast of its enthusiasts that it can easily carry an adult shepherd all day over the Welsh hills.

The Section C is a cross between a Section B and a Section D (logically enough) or the result of two Section C matings. It is not unknown for a Section B-bred animal who grows too big for its section to be registered in Section C of the Welsh stud book (quite legally) and for a Section D showing more pony than cob type (here we go again!) to be similarly treated. To look at, Section Cs are like sturdy ponies or small, finer cobs, and are not more than 14.2 hands high.

Finally, we have the Section D or famous Welsh Cob. These magnificent animals are famed, possibly above all, for their flamboyant, high-speed trotting ability, the spectacle of 'The Trotting of the Cobs' drawing spectators from far and wide at the annual Royal Welsh Show. Like many native breeds, good Welsh Cobs are very hardy, kind-natured and have comfortable paces, and would make ideal first horses for a family. There is no official upper limit to the height of the Welsh Cob, although most of the best seem to be about 15 – 15.1 hands high.

Highland pony
The Highland pony is another animal suitable for all the family. Hailing from Scotland, it ranges from 13 to 14.2 hands and many readers will have seen pictures of them carrying stags down from the mountains after a day's stalking. They are strong, jump freely and can turn their hands to virtually anything. They normally have lovely temperaments and comfortable paces.

New Forest pony
Often confusing to newcomers to the horse world, its name gives the impression that it is born and raised in the forest of that name in Hampshire. However nowadays the New Forest is full of Heinz ponies fighting for survival in an overgrazed, fenced-off environment, many in poor condition and frequently the victims of hit-and-run drivers. One rarely sees a good, pedigree New Forest pony out in the Forest and with good reason – as with any pedigree animal of any species, they can be quite valuable and would quickly become ridden with worms, or stolen, if grazed in the open Forest. Its name does indicate its ancient origins, however, and this breed is, again, suitable for all the family, being a substantial, quality pony up to about 14.2 hands high.

Lundy pony
There is a pony called the Lundy pony which is a very new breed of New Forest stock, found on Lundy Island in the Bristol Channel. A little blood of other sources has been mixed with it and, through living in virtual isolation on the island, the Lundy pony has, over the course of only a few generations and through natural selection and evolution, become a recognized type. Good specimens are well worth having, but there are not many of them around.

Exmoor and Dartmoor ponies
Still in the south of Britain, two small natives with characters and types all their own are the Exmoor, characterized above all by his 'mealy' or beige-coloured muzzle, and the Dartmoor. Their names indicate their origins and purebreds are, indeed, tough customers able to live out; they make good children's riding ponies.

Fell and Dales ponies
Moving north, we have two breeds – the small Fell pony from the Lake District and the larger, heavier Dales pony from Yorkshire. The Dales has had considerable helpings of heavier, larger blood introduced in the past, although the two breeds are from the same foundation stock.

The Fell was developed from local and Scottish stock as a pack pony and general farm pony, often being yoked two or three at a time to a plough. They should not exceed 14 hands in height and are grand ponies, not coarse today as in the past, and well worth considering.

The Dales, as indicated, are a little larger and chunkier than the Fell. They should not exceed 14.2 hands high. Old photographs show some very coarse, big-headed, Roman-nosed individuals, but today's Dales are better-looking, less 'hairy' round the legs (always an indication of cold or carthorse blood somewhere in the past), and are noted particularly for their tolerance of and willingness to work in severe winter weather, as well as for their powerful action.

Shetland pony
The famous, or should I say infamous, Shetland was at one time universally recommended to introduce small children to riding. They are measured in inches rather than hands and should not be more than 42 inches high at four years of age. However, they are

very wide ponies across the back and are not so popular as they once were because of the difficulty of getting small legs down their sides. They are also very strong ponies, inclined to be wilful, although to be fair it should be said that, being used for tiny children, Shetlands are almost always subjected to novice, fairly helpless riders who are totally unable to control them and, being ignorant of even a semblance of good horsemanship, possibly inclined to abuse them, too. The ponies exert their dominance and a bad reputation is born. Today, Shetlands are particularly in favour as driving ponies, but, provided the individual animal is selected carefully, there is no reason why one should not make a good child's pony.

Connemara pony
The final native to be considered is the Connemara pony. It is inaccurate and, indeed, unfair to include it as a British native pony as it is Irish to the core, originating in the wild, windswept southwest of Eire. There is a British breed society for Connemaras, and the breed is very popular as it does make a fine family pony. The Irish Connemara is between 13 and 14 hands but the English one is allowed to grow to 14.2 hands high (ostensibly because it gets better food and grass over here!), although, as with many breeds of any kind, many good examples are to be found outside the height limits. It is only in the 'purist' show classes that height must be adhered to, and performance classes of all types often find under- and oversized natives competing and succeeding with vigour and panache. Connemaras, as with most of our native breeds, performed a wide variety of jobs in the early days of the breed, and are now adaptable animals with cheeky, lovable personalities.

Non-native breeds
Apart from our native breeds of horse and pony, there have been many imports into these islands over the centuries. The 'official' natives themselves probably crossed to this northwest tip of Europe from the continental mainland before the land dropped to form the English Channel, and developed from then on. It is believed that as long ago as the Roman occupation, Arab, or at least oriental horses, were being imported by our conquerors, and, if orientals, why not others? Our famous heavy breeds (not included in my survey as they are certainly not riding or driving horses in the sense being considered here) probably stemmed from a gigantic heavy horse of which the earliest traces have been
32

found in eastern Europe. Our world-famous English Thoroughbred is a true amalgam of oriental and native, already existing
stock, but there are various gaps in early General Stud Book
records (the stud book registering all Thoroughbreds) so no one
can now be really certain of the absolute origins of this superb
speed machine.

More recently, continental warmbloods of various breeds have
been imported. They are called warmbloods because, although
they have some, and in many cases a good deal of, Thoroughbred
blood in them, they also possess other blood from their European
homelands. The main ones are the *Holstein*, the *Hanoverian*, the
Trakhener, the *Westphalian*, the *Danish* and *Swedish* warmbloods
and the *Dutch*. There are also *Norwegian Haflinger* ponies, *Caspians*
(like miniature Thoroughbreds), *Polish* and *Hungarian* breeds,
and a few *French Anglo-Arabs* which are a recognized breed with a
stud book of their own in France, whereas in Britain Anglo-Arabs
are mainly straight crosses between Thoroughbreds and Arabs.
All these are from Europe. In the past, too, though not so much
recently, *Argentinian polo ponies* (again a type and not a breed,
although many were Thoroughbred) were imported, and there
are also some lovely American imports in the *Quarter Horse*, the
Appaloosa and the *Morgan*.

In a nutshell, there is a horse or pony in Britain for everyone, no
matter what their abilities or requirements. Details of breed
society addresses are given in Appendix A at the back of this
book; breed societies are always most willing to send you full
details of their breed and most will put you in touch with
someone who can help you find a suitable animal. Whether you
want a purebred of any breed, a cross of known pedigree (and
there are many excellent animals of this type) or simply a trusty
but competent mixture type – and there are plenty of those, too –
it should not be too difficult to find. Finding your horse will be
discussed in Chapter 5; for now, rest assured that there are plenty
to choose from.

2. Management Systems

In Chapter 1 we discussed the type of accommodation you will be able to offer your horse and also the types and breeds of horse and pony available. The two are closely linked because, to be realistic, the type of accommodation you have available, or can obtain, could determine the kind of horse you get. For example, if all you can find is a safe field with reasonable shelter but, for the foreseeable future, no stable, it is no use buying a Thoroughbred or Arab, or their cross, the Anglo-Arab, or even an animal containing much of these breeds, because such thin-skinned, fine-coated breeds are not happy to live out all year round in the British climate. On the other hand, if you can obtain a stable but not, at present, anywhere to turn out your horse to exercise himself, it is no use buying a horse with lots of nervous energy who is raring to go all the time unless you can give him plenty of work – at least two hours every day. Consideration of the management systems under which horses are kept is therefore vital, so that you can discover what is available in your area and can decide on an appropriate breed or type of horse accordingly.

There are three main systems of keeping a horse – stabled, at grass or on what is called the combined system, where the horse spends part of his time at grass and part stabled. Where grazing is uncommon, horses are also frequently yarded, i.e. kept in dirt enclosures or covered yards or buildings and, because there is no grass, fed as stabled horses. In Britain this method is unusual, but it is used successfully in other countries. It is something we could adopt here with considerable advantage at times when turning out is impossible because of excessively wet land, for example, or

34

when flies are bad in summer. All methods have some advantages and disadvantages, so let us look at them now.

Keeping a Horse Stabled

This is the most expensive and time-consuming method. The
stabled horse is completely at the mercy of his human attendants
– he is, in effect, a prisoner, relying utterly on us for his every
need. He cannot eat or drink unless we provide food and water,
and he cannot take exercise without our riding, driving, lungeing
or leading him. He cannot communicate with other horses unless
we stable him so that he has contact with them or can at least see
them. So you can see that the responsibility on us, and the calls
on our time, are considerable.

However, in winter it is easier to keep a stabled horse warm,
even if he is clipped, than an outdoor one, because we can put on
blankets and rugs and protect him from the weather inside his
stable, even with the top door of his box open, as it normally
should be. This alone will save to some extent on food bills, since
keeping warm is one of the primary uses of food.

From the point of view of time, this method is the least
economical. The stabled horse has got to be exercised by us. A
reasonably fit, healthy horse needs a good two hours' exercise
every day as a minimum. Even if we have access to a mechanical
horsewalker which will walk or trot horses round and round in
circles for as long as we wish, this form of exercise can be
unacceptably boring to the horse if carried out for more than half
an hour, so human time has to be spent exercising him.

The stable has to be mucked out (droppings and dirty bedding
removed) and bedded down with fresh bedding, and at half an
hour a time, twice a day, this amounts to another hour a day. The
horse's skin has to be kept clean by grooming as it is not being
rained on, and this takes at least another thirty minutes to one
hour daily. The reason for keeping horses stabled is usually
because they can be made fitter for hard work under this system,
so the skin, which is important in excretion of toxins and in heat
regulation, has to be kept in optimum condition – clean,
stimulated and working at peak efficiency. Here we have yet
further grounds for having to give a thorough daily grooming.

The advantages of stabling are that the horse is always handy,
dry and reasonably clean when we want him. We can control his
diet down to the last grain or cube and so, combining this with

35

correct exercise, can bring him to the peak of fitness for whatever hard work we want to give him. It has to be admitted, even by the most diehard back-to-nature supporters, that many horses love their stables, especially in wet, windy weather and when the sun and flies become unbearable in summer. Even in cold, dry, still weather, which most horses don't mind at all, they like to come in at night to a good feed and a thick, dry bed. Horses usually regard their stables as their home base, their 'pad', their personal space, and, unless we give them reason to feel otherwise, feel secure there.

The disadvantages for the horse are that this home base can truly seem like a prison if his human attendants do not let or take him out enough. Horses are by nature nomadic animals and need to be kept moving for both physical and mental health. Provided ample exercise is given, however, keeping a horse stabled, particularly in poor weather, can be quite acceptable to him.

Keeping a Horse at Grass

This method is probably the most misunderstood of all. On the face of it it seems like an idyllic existence – the horse is free to roam, provided the field is big enough, or at least to walk about and keep his body moving as nature intended. He can gallop, buck and kick in play or high spirits – the latter two, at least, being normally prohibited in working conditions – and can enjoy the sun on his back and the taste of grass, nature's own self-contained food. If he is with other horses, he can enjoy normal social relations with them and be as close to nature as domestication allows.

In practice, however, things can be very different. If the field is small and/or there are too many horses on it (see Chapter 3), the grass can be eaten away to such an extent that he cannot get enough of it and becomes hungry. It can become contaminated with droppings, near which horses will not graze, which cuts down further the area available. If the weather is bad – cold, wind and wet are the outdoor horse's three worst enemies in winter – he can suffer considerably physically and mentally, losing weight as his body tries to ward off the effects of the weather and keep warm, and he can develop exposure ailments such as rain scald and mud fever.

Extremes of summer weather are just as bad. Lack of shade in hot weather can cause considerable discomfort, and flies can
36

make horses' lives a living hell. I feel many people completely disregard or underestimate the suffering caused by flies irritating the horse's most sensitive areas such as eyes (especially), sheath and dock, and wish to stress that the horse's natural defences against them are, in practice, pathetically inadequate.

Even if we allow the horse to grow a long enough mane and forelock to be of any use when he shakes his head, the flies only take off for a second or two; then they are back. His tail can be flicked to reach flies on the rear half of the body, and the flat muscle under the skin of shoulders and flanks can be twitched to remove the little beasts from in-between areas, but again, the effect is very temporary, and the continual use of these defences is wearing in the extreme. Horses are often ultimately driven to galloping around their field – at this speed the flies cannot keep up with them. Galloping can, however, only be resorted to for a comparative short period of time and has its own dangers. The heart and lungs can be overstressed, exhaustion can occur and, if the ground is hard, as it often is in summer, feet and legs can be badly jarred. Unshod hooves can also chip away and the horses become footsore.

So from the horse's point of view the outdoor life is often far from idyllic. The only times of year when reasonable conditions are likely to occur are spring and autumn – and in spring young, rich grass can cause digestive troubles and obesity, not to mention the dreaded laminitis (see Chapter 8).

Many of these disadvantages can be overcome by providing proper shelter for the horses in the form of an open-fronted shed (see Chapter 3), but owners without their own facilities may simply have to take what they can get, and it has to be admitted that fields with any sheds at all, let alone adequate ones, seem to be woefully rare. (See illustration.)

From the owner's point of view, the advantages of keeping the horse at grass are that, although reasonably regular hours have to be kept, we are not so tied down to the last half hour as we are with a stabled horse. If we really do not have time to work the outdoor horse, it does not matter since he can give himself enough exercise to maintain his health. He will also, hopefully, have at least a reasonable amount of grazing available, so he should never get really hungry except possibly in winter when the grass has very little nutriment in it.

Time is also saved on mucking out the stable, since there isn't one, although droppings have to removed daily from a shelter if we wish to prevent it's becoming an indoor muckheap. In addition outdoor horses do not need – indeed must not have – the thorough grooming of the stabled horse, because they need the natural grease in their coats to give at least some protection from the weather.

The disadvantages are that grass-kept horses are often wet and muddy when you go to catch them up for work, and, if your time is limited, you can often not get them dry enough to put tack on in the time you have available. For most of the year you cannot get a grass-kept horse quite as clean and smart-looking as a stabled one, nor quite so supremely fit (but see Chapter 8). In addition, some horses develop the infuriating habit of being hard to catch, particularly if turned out with one who is already accomplished at evading capture.

Unless there is a shed or overhead cover of some sort available, you may often have to minister to your horse in lashing rain and howling gales, neither easy nor pleasant, and may have the added inconvenience of having to transport feed, hay, straw,

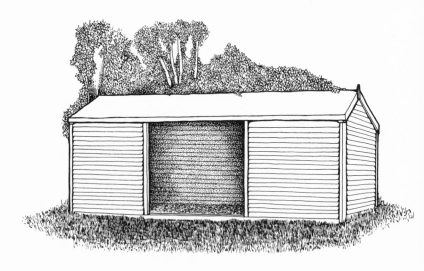

A sturdy field shelter. Although the front has a wide entrance, this design provides overhead and side protection whatever the direction of the wind. With completely open-fronted sheds, the wind can sometimes blow right in. Shelters forming three-quarters of a circle are the safest sort, although very rarely seen, as horses cannot be hemmed into a corner by other occupants

waterproof rugs, harness or tack and other paraphernalia to a possibly inaccessible plot, down a track ankle-deep in mud and with, needless to say, no lighting facilities.

If you can sort out a decent field, acceptably convenient, you may well feel that, given the right sort of animal (half-Thorough-bred/Arab, cob or native type), keeping a horse at grass is all right for your circumstances, but do be aware that it is neither very cheap nor trouble-free. Grass-kept animals in winter have to be fed extra to keep out the cold and, in their own way, can require as much expenditure of time on your part, depending on the location of the field, as a stabled horse.

Combined System

I have to admit that this is my favourite system of horse-keeping as it can offer the best of both worlds to both horse and owner. The horse can have the comfort of his stable and the freedom of his field, because he regularly uses them both.

The normal method is for the horse to be out all or part of the day in winter and in at night, and the other way round in summer, but this is a very general description because the exact lengths of time depend on your circumstances and the horse's preferences and constitution. Most horses tell their attendants very plainly when they want to come in by standing round the gate, hoping that someone will come and get them. It is, as already mentioned, not only cold, driving rain and wind that makes them want stabling but also excessive sun, heat and insects.

A proper shelter shed in the field is an excellent precaution against leaving a horse out against his wishes, for both grass-kept and combined-system animals. Despite what you may be told to the contrary, horses and ponies do use them when they feel the need, unless they are being kept out by a bully horse, or because they are frightened for some other reason such as the shelter being too low or dark or the approach being badly poached into a morass of liquid mud.

The combined system is ideal for working owners who simply haven't the time or desire to exercise their horses before and after work. They can do the early morning chores which might take half an hour, then, instead of having to set off on an hour's exercise, can simply turn the horse out for the day, bringing him in after work in the evening. In summer, they will probably be

39

bringing the horse in in the morning so he can lie and rest during the day after walking about grazing all night, then turn him out again, perhaps after exercise, in the evening.

You may hear a lot of excuses from other horse owners as to why they do not turn out their horses. A very common one is: 'He might hurt himself in the field – he always gallops about.' In fact, he is much more likely to get hurt at work than in the field, and if he gallops about a lot it is probably because he is not used to it and is overwhelmed by the exhilaration of being free. If he were turned out regularly he would be much more sensible.

Another excuse is: 'He'll get dirty.' What an unkind reason for keeping a horse cooped up! Obviously an owner will want to keep a horse clean before some important occasion, but at other times, if spotless cleanliness is considered so important, why not throw on a lightweight New Zealand (waterproof) rug? It is far better to keep the horse happy than immaculate!

A third excuse is: 'He always jumps out.' If he is alone, he might well jump out looking for company, so the answer to that is clear. If he is an inveterate jumper-outer, probably the fencing is not all it should be (see Chapter 3) so, again, the answer is obvious.

The final most common, and very strange, excuse is: 'Grass is bad for him when he's working.' This is simply not true unless the grazing is very rich – most unusual in paddocks used for horses – and he is out on it for several hours. It is true that rich grazing can cause digestive and circulatory problems and excessive weight gain, which are undesirable in a working horse particularly, but even an hour's freedom a day is better than nothing.

Grass does, in practice, seem to help the digestion of other foods and horses certainly enjoy it. Even if turning out is not possible, ten or fifteen minutes' grazing on the end of a leadrope should be given daily. Turning out your horse not only takes some of the weight off the shoulders of a busy owner who has restricted time for exercise; the fact that the horse is exercising himself helps keep him fitter than if he were left to stagnate in his stable, and relieves the boredom which this can cause.

As this is your first horse, I would strongly recommend that you make life easier for both yourself and your horse by keeping him somewhere where he can be on the combined system. This will give you both the best of both worlds.

Yarding

The fourth system, yarding, allows the horse some freedom, keeps him easily available, also clean if he is under cover, and allows control of the diet as he will not be grazing – although, as mentioned, grass is usually more of a help to digestion than a hindrance. The flooring of an open yard may be sand, which is good, or soil, which will become mud in wet weather. Surfaces such as cinders and slag are often disliked by horses, however. The best yards are at least partly covered, the area under cover often being bedded on wood shavings, sawdust, peat, sand or a mixture of these. Horses happily lie and rest here and can come in and go out as they wish. Unfortunately, as mentioned earlier, such facilities are rare in Britain.

Other Considerations

You will also have to decide whether you are going to keep your horse at home, in rented accommodation or at full or part livery. As ever, there are pros and cons to each method, but for a first-time owner I feel that the first year should be spent with the horse *at livery* in a good establishment, even if other facilities might be available and cheaper. The reason for this is that it will give you a whole year's experience of keeping a horse in all weather conditions with reliable, probably qualified supervision and attention on hand. Advice will be readily and freely forthcoming, and there will be many occasions when you need it in these early days. You will have the advantage of absorbing the atmosphere of a well-run establishment and will learn a great deal about stable management if you take an interest in how the other horses, with all their individual quirks, are cared for in sickness and health. All this will give you a good grounding for when you are sufficiently experienced and knowledgeable to take over full responsibility for your horse yourself.

Simply keeping a horse in *rented accommodation* (often called *do-it-yourself livery*) does not have the same advantages. The owners of such yards frequently seem unwilling to involve themselves in any way in the care or wellbeing of your horse. Advice may be given grudgingly, if at all, and may not be of the best because the proprietor feels that the horse is your sole responsibility. After all, he reasons, you are only paying for the use of his facilities – the rest is up to you. There are exceptions to this, but generally

41

first-timers would be well advised to pay a bit extra, even for only part livery, and have the peace of mind of knowing that help and advice are there when needed.

Most reputable establishments will require you to sign a livery contract setting out various terms such as the exact services you are paying for, the price, insurance aspects and whether or not they are to be allowed the use of your horse, if it is a riding/driving school. This is for your good as well as theirs, and every section must be gone through in detail, clarified in writing where necessary, and each side given a copy. Of course, you will be much happier with people you can talk to and with whom you can develop a friendly business relationship rather than one which is purely commercial and somewhat mercenary, but this you will only discover with time, so you will have to be guided by early impressions. Choosing an establishment is covered in Chapter 3, but now let's have a look at your contract with the livery stable.

First, the size of stable should be stipulated to avoid any subjective opinion over what is 'big enough' or 'too small'. For an animal of about 15 hands high, I should regard 12 feet square as a minimum size. The box has to be large enough for the horse to turn round in comfort and for him to lie down and get up in safety. Horses sleep lying flat out with their head and legs stretched full out, so the box must be big enough to permit this. They also doze lying down on their bellies, with their legs tucked under them.

As to height, 7 feet 6 inches to the eaves, if the roof is a ridge roof/double plane, or 10 feet to the lowest part if a single-plane, sloping roof should be offered. The doorway should be not less than 4 feet wide and 7 feet 6 inches high. If there is a window, it should have a protective grille on the inside to prevent the horse breaking it and injuring himself.

Do ensure that your horse has the sort of stable door which has top and bottom leaves, so that the top can normally be left open and fastened back. This allows him a view of the world and helps with ventilation. You may not get all these details in your agreement, but you must know what to look for so that you can decide what is really adequate.

Secondly, the agreement should state that your livery fee includes daily turning-out facilities, if you wish. Then if the proprietor refuses to turn out your horse you can point to the agreement and at least request a refund. Land has to be rested and managed, but any decent establishment will work out a rota so that this can be accomplished while still reserving some land for turning out. You may have to cooperate, again on a rota system, over length of time out, but try to stipulate that you get a certain number of hours daily if you want them.

Thirdly, determine what services you want. These have been detailed earlier, so decide which you require and make sure they are in your contract. Then, if you find you are paying for both turning out and ridden exercise but your horse is getting only one of them, again you have grounds for taking up the matter with the proprietor.

Feeding should also be covered, although horses' requirements differ according to work and time of year. Discuss the matter in depth with the proprietor and get it stipulated that the horse is to be fed sufficiently to keep him in good condition for his circumstances. Unfortunately this is very much a matter of opinion, but as with experience you become a better judge of physical condition, you will know whether your horse is being fed properly or not. If any dispute arises, a vet or other expert should be approached to give a professional opinion on the horse's condition. This would be unusual because any reputable establishment will make sure – for the sake of its reputation if nothing else – that horses there are kept looking well! The fact is that if nothing is laid down in your agreement, you haven't a leg to stand on if things do go wrong.

Regarding health and sickness, you should have a clause in your contract which ensures that you are contacted immediately should the horse become sick or receive any injury other than something very minor. The clause should authorize the proprietor to call in your vet (or another if he or she is unavailable) without previously contacting you, should circumstances warrant it. Immediate attention could save a horse's life; delays while a livery proprietor tries in vain to contact a horse's owner can have disastrous results.

Expenses not to be covered by your fees must be laid out, and will commonly include shoeing, veterinary attention, cost of worming medicines and items of tack and grooming kit. Mucking out tools are normally those of the stable, but again, do establish what is covered and what is not – in writing. Remember that actual schooling, as opposed to correct riding while exercising, will cost extra.

If the livery centre is to have the use of your horse in exchange for a fee reduction – a situation often fraught with difficulties – stipulate that he is only used by experienced people under expert

43

supervision and is available when you want him. If you are going to ride mainly at weekends, just when the centre will need him most, you could find this sort of arrangement untenable in your case; but again, do get everything clear.

Although the centre will have its own insurance policies covering accidents and 'professional indemnity' in case of the inevitable element of 'human error', they will surely require that you, too, have your own policy. This topic is discussed in Chapter 4.

Whatever kind of livery service you have, full or part, you can arrange an appropriate contract to suit both you and the proprietor, with a little discussion and common sense give and take. No agreement is final – it can always be changed in the light of different circumstances – but some kind of contract there certainly should be.

Even when keeping horses in rented accommodation with no services, you should have a contract which details the facilities you are paying for, so that your horse cannot be turfed out of his box into a hovel or prevented from being turned out. In this situation you will need somewhere to store your feed as you will have to buy your own, and somewhere secure for your tack and other equipment – you cannot take it all home with you every day.

If you decide to keep your horse at home despite everything, remember you may well be completely on your own regarding help and advice. Even in a DIY yard, there is usually some other owner willing to give help and information, and you can build up friendships with like-minded people. At home this does not happen, so you have to be very sure of your capabilities before taking the plunge.

Unless your family is going to help you, you will also have to handle the workload on your own, and it can be considerable. If you are ill or injured, who will look after the horse? What about your holidays? The horse will still need looking after and cannot just be left in a field to fend for himself while you are away. Can you make alternative arrangements in such cases? Also, what about feed deliveries? Most feed companies require someone to sign for consignments on delivery. Will there be someone who knows nuts from grain who can accept delivery in your absence at work? If not, you could be faced with collecting your own supplies, a considerable inconvenience.

On the credit side, there is nothing quite so heartwarming than to be able to step outside your own back door and hear your horse

44

whinnying a welcome. You can have him under close, personal supervision and know that your wishes for his management are being carried out properly because you are doing everything yourself. You will certainly find it cheaper as there are no fees or rent to pay, and the horse will be truly one of the family, being in frequent close contact with all of you every day.

Only you can decide what method of keeping your horse is right for you according to your circumstances, your locality and your bank balance. Knowing the pros and cons, however, will help you to make the correct decision on this very important topic.

3. Finding Accommodation

It may be that you have already decided to keep your new horse, for a while at least, at the school you already attend. If you have been a satisfied client there, are on good terms with the proprietor and staff and are happy with the facilities they can provide, this could be an excellent arrangement.

If you are not fixed up, however, this chapter should help you find a suitable home for your horse. First, we'll discuss what to look for in facilities, so you can tell the suitable from the unsuitable or downright dangerous.

The stable

Size has been mentioned already, so a word now about ventilation. Horses are athletic animals needing healthy lungs, and lungs cannot work well if they spend most of their time in a stale, unhealthy atmosphere. They need fresh air – and it is quite possible to provide this without exposing the horse to draughts or an excessively cold atmosphere provided the ventilation in the stable is correct.

Most horses in Britain are kept in loose boxes (called box stalls in America). These are 'single rooms', if you like, with two-leaf doors opening to the outside. Unless the wind is blowing directly into the box on a cold day, it is normally best to leave the top door open so that the horse can put his head out and air can get in.

There may well be a window, which is needed for light and ventilation on those occasions when the door happens to be shut. The usual type is called the Sheringham, which opens upward
46

and inward, ostensibly to direct the flow of air up over the horse's back. It is obvious, however, that when the top door is open, creating what amounts to a gaping hole in the wall, any niceties about the airflow from the window can be disregarded. It is another form of ventilation, however, and should normally be open.

I feel that not enough stables have ridge-roof ventilators to let out the stale warm air which always rises, nor wall louvre ventilators. Look for them, as they are a definite advantage. The type of ventilation you certainly don't want is gaps in the boards and missing bricks, which will place your horse in a constant draught from which he cannot escape. A horse in a sizeable, properly ventilated stable can position himself away from any direct airflow from the door or window if he wants to, but draughts coming from gaps low down in the structure are difficult to escape – and unlike a horse in a field, he cannot move around to keep warm. For the same reason there should not be a yawning gap under the bottom of the door. (See illustration.)

A simple, practical test of the ventilation is to spend some time outdoors, then go into an occupied box. Breathe in and notice whether there is any noticeable difference in the smell and feel of the air from that outside. If you notice any significant difference, such as a very strong smell of horse, mugginess, mustiness, or, worse, the acid/ammonia type of smell given off by urine, and if the air feels considerably warmer than that outside, the ventilation is simply not good enough.

Another good stabling system is the American barn system, where loose boxes are sited inside a large building, normally down the outside walls leaving a central aisle. Such boxes have sliding doors opening to the aisle and sometimes doors at the other side leading outside, too. Two exits are useful in case of fire in such a building, and in any case it is good for the horse to have two views, one outside and one inside. In countries experiencing extremes of climate, such as the U S A, the outside doors can be left closed as well as the large sliding doors at either end of the barn, helping to keep the animal warm.

The final system, not so common nowadays except in military and some police yards, is to keep horses permanently tied up in 6-foot-wide stalls. Although most private owners, including the author, would prefer their horse to have the freedom of a loose box, the system does work well with horses of quiet temperament who do much more work than the average private horse.

The structure of the stable, whatever kind, must be strong

47

since horses, and even small ponies, are very strong animals which are easily able to kick their way through a single brick or wooden wall. Most won't, and those who do usually do so from boredom through being inside too long, but the possibility should be borne in mind. Brick stables are best; stone is good, if cold in winter; and concrete blocks – not compressed ash breeze blocks – are also strong. Double-skinned wood is quite good and very common, and any stable is improved by wooden lining, even if only halfway up to form so-called kicking boards to help protect the structure if the horse does kick.

Insulation is important, and for this reason metal and asbestos are not recommended for any part of a horse's accommodation. The roof should be made of any material which is a poor conductor of heat. Double-skinned wood under roofing felt is good, as are slates or tiles. The addition of polystyrene tiles or sheeting on the inside will aid insulation.

The floor should be non-slip because, even if it is covered with bedding, some horses paw and expose the floor, and metal shoes on a slippery surface are highly dangerous. Concrete is a very common flooring material but one of the worst. It may not be slippery, but it absorbs water and urine and is cold and hard. Wood is useless – it is slippery when wet, absorbent, and breaks up easily. Asphalt is excellent, but uncommon. It is softer than concrete and if the loose-weave type is used over rubble, urine drains away through it, helping to save bedding. Old-fashioned, ridged stable bricks are now hard to come by and expensive, and, despite what the old books say, they can be very slippery.

Just on the market at the time of writing is a product called the Ridry Stable Flooring system, described as 'a strong perforated platform laid under the bedding which allows moisture to pass through'. This should certainly save bedding and provide a resilient, non-slip underlayer, but care would be needed with drainage to prevent urine simply pooling under it. It would seem good for stables with central drains (notorious for becoming blocked with bedding) and for those sloping slightly (but not so much that you'd notice!) towards an outlet at the bottom of the wall, the idea being that the urine runs away to outside drains.

Not often recommended but quite feasible in practice are floors made simply of soil, fine compressed shale and the like. Bedding is simply laid on top and urine and any spilled water just drains through the ground. This may sound horrific to the purists, but I kept my horse for a whole winter in such a box and he was fine. Some horses do dig in these floors, which then have to be repaired, but owners who like them say the advantages to the horses' legs from being on a softish surface are well worth the odd repair.

Old-fashioned cobbles are only good as a base for laying some other flooring material. They present an uneven, highly uncomfortable surface to the horse's feet, detectable even through bedding. Excessively sloped floors, too, should be avoided or evened up, or else the horse will always be standing uncomfortably. Concrete blocks (again, not weak breeze blocks) can form a fair floor if laid onto a foundation of deep gravel with a half-inch drainage gap between them.

All stable floors should be a few inches above ground level, otherwise water from the yard will run in and soak the bedding. Local by-laws may insist that you have 'properly drained' stables,

A row of pre-fabricated timber looseboxes, very commonly seen. Although they could be higher (at extra cost!) the horses do have adequate headroom and the boxes have both ridge-roof and gable-end louvre ventilators. The overhang provides welcome protection from sun, wind and rain. The mounting block is a useful feature not so often seen nowadays, which makes mounting easier for both humans (at least the less agile ones) and horses. One simply 'steps' over the horse's back and so avoids any possibility of the saddle being pulled over, at some discomfort to the horse, when weight is put on the nearside stirrup

49

which may mean considerable expense. In practice, provided the box is on dry standing they are not essential, as most urine will be soaked up by the bedding; however, slightly sloped floors with drainage channels running to an outside drain will help satisfy your local authority and help a little with bedding. The things to avoid are low, flat floors which hold moisture.

Some stables opening directly outdoors have a roof overhang of about 3 or 4 feet, which protects horses from wind, rain and sun. It also protects their attendants somewhat – a welcome feature in the English winter!

Stable Fittings
You will probably need some items termed 'stable fittings' in your box. These comprise a manger, hayrack, ring for tying up a haynet if you have no rack (which can double for tying up the horse, when necessary), maybe an automatic waterer or a holder for a water bucket, electric light and switch, door bolts and a window grille. These things are by no means essential, but are most useful.

The important point to remember is that the inside of a stable should be as smooth as possible with no projections on which the horse could hurt himself. Hayracks (made of strong metal bars) should be the type which fit across a corner and should be fitted with the top a few inches above the horse's ears, high enough to help prevent his knocking his head on them but not so high that bits fall in his eyes while he is eating.

The manger, metal or polythene, should likewise be fitted across a corner with the top just a little higher than the horse's elbows. The bottom edge of the manger should be rounded off to prevent injury to his knees if he stamps while feeding. Some boxes have built-in mangers with the space beneath bricked or boarded up, and a cupboard for grooming kit incorporated into the space.

The ring mentioned should be bolted securely through an outside wall, with a metal plate between the outside nut and wall, to prevent the horse pulling it through (a horse can exert a pull of one and a half times his own weight). Bolts for the door should be sited at top and bottom (a) as a belt-and-braces precaution and (b) to prevent the bottom of the door being pushed outwards should the horse lie against it, providing a gap through which he could get a foot, with disastrous results. The bottom bolt could, for convenience, be one of the foot-operated type.

The field

Fields used for horses are often the poor relations when it comes to land use. They should be well drained – no clumps of spiky marsh grasses – and preferably slightly sloping towards a ditch or other outlet, otherwise they will be out of use for much of the year in Britain. The grass should be of medium to poor quality – surprisingly, maybe, but more about this in Chapter 8 – with no poisonous plants or excessive weeds.

Fencing should be strong and safe and at least up to the height of the horses' backs, in other words 4 feet 6 inches to 5 feet. Anything lower will not deter those fond of jumping out. Thick, prickly hedging is the best barrier. (See illustration.)

Post and rail fencing in a paddock is the next best thing to thick, natural hedges as far as safety goes, but obviously gives no shelter. The top rail (which should be flush with the tops of the posts, as shown) should be the height of the horses' backs and the second rail the height of their elbows. This type of post and rail fencing is much more economical than the more usual three- or four-rail type and quite adequate for mature horses. Breeding stock should have four-rail fencing. The posts should be on the outside of the fencing, as shown, to prevent possible shoulder injuries. Where one fence serves as two paddocks a single rail at shoulder height should be run along the other side of the posts to present a smooth barrier

51

Barbed wire should never be used for horses, though it is regrettably common in rented 'spare grazing' procured on farms. Horses can gallop along or into it, or get their legs caught, resulting in terrible injuries. Wooden posts and rails are good, and plain wire kept tightly strained between wooden posts is also good. Various proprietary brands of fencing are now available, such as flexible plastic, diamond mesh wire and square mesh wire, with the lower meshes too small to allow a horse's hoof through. Details can be obtained by answering advertisements in equestrian magazines.

General safety in the field is also important. Here are a number of points to watch.

The ground should not be very rough or have holes in it – such hazards are dangerous to galloping horses who can trip and fall or put their legs into a hole and break them. There should be no farm implements or machinery left in the field – harrows hidden in the grass are particularly dangerous as horses canter right onto them, piercing their hooves.

Litter such as glass bottles or tin cans, thrown into the field by passers-by, and also plastic feed or fertilizer sacks, are dangerous and frightening respectively. Fields with rights of way through them are not ideal as they provide unhindered access to vandals and marauding pet dogs.

Ponds and dykes should really be fenced off. Horses can fall into dykes and die of exhaustion trying to get out, or can drown if they land on their backs (yes, this does happen), and ponds often consist of stagnant or polluted water. They frequently have unsafe approaches and in winter, if they freeze over, horses can wander onto the ice and fall in. Streams with gravel or stony bottoms can provide a good water source if you are sure the water is unpolluted and, again, if the approach is safe. Streams with sandy bottoms are said to be unsuitable as sand taken in with the water can cause colic.

Field gates can be a source of danger, too. They should be smooth and strong, like the fencing: wooden-railed gates or tubular metal ones are usually good. As horses congregate round gates, and mill around when they want to come in, the bottom halves of gates should be filled in with strong metal mesh, safely fixed. Gate fastenings should be of the type unable to be opened by horses and recessed into the gate, to prevent injury, or a headcollar getting caught.

Sliprails are a cheap and acceptable alternative to gates, but one end of each pole should be bolted through its receiving post and the other end in a closed-top holder to prevent some crafty individual getting his neck underneath and nudging it along until it falls down, letting him out. It is surprising what our supposedly dim horses can get up to!

Other Facilities

Storage areas are also needed for feed (which ideally should be kept in galvanized bins or hoppers to guard against vermin, although many people use tough plastic dustbins to good effect), for hay (which must be kept out of the weather to avoid wastage), for bedding and for tack and harness. Dry, airy conditions are needed for feed, and for convenience feed rooms should be near the stables.

Tack is very expensive and attractive to thieves; therefore it should be kept in a securely lockable building in dry, not too cold conditions. A touch of luxury is to have a thermostatically controlled heater in the tack room, keeping it at about 20°C. Otherwise mildew will soon rot everything.

The siting of the muck heap is important. For obvious reasons it should be downwind of the stables and house, so look at trees in the area to see in which direction the prevailing wind bends them. Much muck disposal these days is carried out by mushroom nurseries who provide metal skips for you to tip the muck into. To save muscular energy these should, if possible, be sited in a dip so that muck can be tipped down rather than heaved up!

Water supplies to stables and field can be supplied by automatic waterers or buckets to the stables, and to the fields by piped troughs or some other safe, large container filled by hosepipe. Much inconvenience is caused through burst pipes in winter, so pipes should be lagged well when above ground or laid 2 feet deep underground. Any pipes and electrical wires in stables should be in metal conduits to prevent the horse interfering with them, and light switches should be waterproof and outside the box, well away from his teeth. The actual light should be similarly well up out of reach and/or have a strong metal guard.

Inspecting Premises

How do you set about finding somewhere suitable for your horse? If you have no idea where to start, I recommend you to contact the British Horse Society and the Association of British Riding Schools, asking them to supply a list of all their officially approved establishments in your area.

These two organizations run fairly strict approval schemes to ensure the safety and welfare of horses, students and staff at their centres, so you should be assured of a good standard of care for your horse. But I am afraid this is not always the case; there are odd cases of approved stables neglecting or even ill-treating animals, but in such cases either a complaint or the annual inspection will uncover them, and the centre will either have to come up to scratch or lose its approval status, which could cost it a lot of money or even put it out of business.

Local authorities have to license riding schools. This is meant to ensure reasonable standards of instruction, safety, facilities and care, as a veterinary inspection is also included. In practice, however, there are many licensed schools which fall far below the standards required for approval by the BHS and ABRS, so the fact that a school advertises itself as 'licensed' does not mean much in many areas.

There is no approval or licensing scheme for livery stables, as opposed to schools, so you have to be guided by your own knowledge and impression. The same goes for establishments renting out accommodation for DIY liveries, accommodation on farms, grazing rented out or similar arrangements. If you cannot find an approved centre within reasonable distance, obtain the name and address of your local BHS representative from the society and ask him or her if they could recommend a good place for your horse to live. Such people often have good local contacts and will know the reputable from the shady. Local newspapers and equestrian journals, both local and national, plus horsey sections of the local farming press, notably *The Farmer's Guardian*, often carry advertisements for livery services and the like, so even though anyone is entitled to place an advertisement with them, at least it will give you some names and addresses to start with.

A word of warning about keeping your horse on a farm. Most modern farmers do not know the first thing about horses! It is not their fault, as horses are very rare on farms these days. However, you will sometimes see stabling and grazing advertised for rent on farms with an element of 'care' thrown in. It is never a good idea to keep a horse with people who know nothing about them, even if you are doing most of the work yourself. Horses are not cows; they do not function like cows, they do not think or behave

54

like cows, and you cannot handle them like cows. Farmers often do not realize this and through ignorant and incorrect management many 'accidents' and illnesses have been suffered by horses kept on farms. I should advise you not to keep your horse at such a place until you are very knowledgeable yourself, and even then only if you are desperate.

Chapter 4 gives advice on finding an expert adviser, which I regard as essential for a prospective first-time owner. For now, I shall simply say that you should always take a person of this kind with you when looking round establishments and be guided by their opinion.

You may have a friend who has offered to keep your horse at his or her home with their family horse or horses. This could be a good arrangement, certainly, but it could also lead to the end of the friendship if, once ensconced, you find that your friend's idea of correct care and management is very different from your own or from what you are fast discovering is to be aimed at. Such arrangements also often mean that your horse will be regarded very much as a third-class citizen, no matter how much you are paying, who will be on the tail end of your friend's attentions and considerations. This may sound cynical, but it does happen a great deal, so take care before entering such an arrangement.

Let us suppose now that you have found somewhere to inspect and are going along to see what it is like – with your expert adviser. It will probably be necessary for you to make an appointment so that someone is available to show you round and answer your queries, not to mention confirming whether or not they can provide what you want. Making an appointment does, of course, give them a chance to tidy up, but no amount of quick clear-ups can hide the signs of persistent neglect and low standards, so this need not deter you.

Try to look at things from your horse's point of view. You do not need to be an expert horsemaster to tell whether horses are too thin, dirty to the skin (as opposed to muddy from rolling in the field), miserable, nasty-tempered (although the odd sourpuss can exist anywhere), wearing filthy rugs and blankets and generally depressed and neglected. In any case, you are not a total novice or you would not be considering buying a horse of your own.

Remember that the horse does not a care a hoot if the paintwork is peeling a bit, if the bolts and hinges on his door are a bit rusty, if the muck heap is a bit of a mess or if the yard needs sweeping. What he would care about would be dark, airless stables, lack of food or poor-quality food (see Chapter 8), holes in the walls, rugs which have slipped round and are uncomfortable, attendants who are rough and uncaring or unknowledgeable, lack of bedding or piles of droppings in his box. I'd much rather keep my horse at a place where he and his friends were considered more important than smartly painted flower tubs and white fencing or sparkling windows.

In short, look very carefully at the horses wherever you go. It is they who will tell you whether they are well cared for (and about) or not. They should have alert, interested expressions, should investigate you with interest, should usually be looking out of their boxes at what is going on rather than standing with their tails to the door, bored and depressed. Their coats should be bright and clean, and you should not be aware that they have ribs and backbones!

Of course, if the buildings are obviously very run down and the place is plainly a tip, this could mean lack of working capital (so feed bills might not be paid, affecting the next delivery) or a shortage of human attendants to run the place adequately. Rotten wood can be dangerous (buildings do fall down sometimes) and excessive untidiness can mean a bit of a slipshod attitude to everything, which might include the horses. Form your own impressions, but after you leave do discuss things with your EA (expert adviser), simply remembering that it is the condition of the horses which should be the main deciding factor.

If you have a choice of several establishments, start with the one nearest your home. Why waste time and travelling expenses if what you want is right round the corner? You can always go further afield if you have to. Of course, it is better to keep your horse 20 miles away in a place where he will be superbly cared for than half a mile away at a place which will be giving you constant worry and sleepless nights over his welfare, even if you don't get to see him quite as often.

Many riding establishments have a large number of students (who may know considerably less than you do) to care for the horses. This is a question of economics – the finances of the British horse world simply do not allow for an all-qualified staff. However, this need not be a disadvantage provided that the students are closely supervised by someone competent. Some yards, in any case, have qualified staff looking after the liveries and use their own horses to give students experience.

Paper qualifications are a guide to their holder's competence, but no more. This does not mean your horse will not be well cared for at a yard where staff are not qualified. It is a difficult question, but again the state of the horses can be your guide.

A Stable at Home

If you do feel you are competent to have your horse at home, you will have to check with your local authority as to their requirements under the Public Health and Safety regulations. They will be concerned about drainage and smells, fire risks (hay and straw are easily flammable) and whether the horse can escape and be a nuisance to neighbours or cause an accident on the roads.

You may feel that your local authority would never allow you to keep your horse at home if you live in a residential area, but in fact they may well be unable to stop you provided that you keep within certain conditions laid down in the Town and Country Planning Act and its subsequent General Development (Amendment) Orders. You must not cause such a nuisance through smells and noise that your neighbours complain, of course; even then you will get a warning first, or should do.

Regulations change, but in 1985 you are allowed to build a stable on your own property and have it regarded as an enlargement of the property, or domestic offices, provided that such a building (classed as an enlargement) does not exceed one-tenth of the cubic content of the original dwelling house, or 50 cubic metres, subject to a maximum of 115 cubic metres. You will have to get sight of the deeds to your property (if you have a mortgage your building society will probably hold them, and will in any case have to be informed) to see if the house and related outbuildings have been enlarged since construction to the extent that your 'allowance' has been used up. This may well be the case if you or a previous owner has had a garage erected, a conservatory built on or some such, so check carefully. Your stable must also not be higher than the highest part of the original dwelling house and should not protrude beyond the front line of the building where it fronts a highway. This might all sound a bit complicated, but the right is there for you to use. Why not talk it over with your solicitor to be certain?

Keeping your horse at home is certainly a feasible proposition, then, even if you have no real grazing, provided you can exercise him enough. You might be able to find grazing reasonably near your home, and simply bring the horse home when stabling is needed, say at night in winter. More than a few garages have been pressed into use as hay and straw stores, while the car has been turfed out into the drive or onto the street.

4. Playing Safe

The purpose of this chapter is to point you in the direction of the various experts who can help you with the technical aspects of buying and owning a horse. I believe wholeheartedly that in such an important transaction it is worth paying for expert help to try to ensure that you end up with a horse suitable for you and your requirements. If, for example, you view a horse alone or with a friend who knows little more than you do, you might fall in love with the horse on sight and not notice some quite obvious fault which could jeopardize his ability or the safety of both of you, not to mention some minor defect which only an expert could spot but which might make the difference between a good buy and a disaster.

For a start, it would be a good idea to write to the Association of British Riding Schools for their comprehensive and informative booklet *The Law on the Buying and Selling of Horses*, which (in 1985) costs only 50p plus a stamped, addressed envelope.

Horse Consultant

Next, make sure you have access to the expert adviser already mentioned who will go with you to inspect the horse, and maybe even find it for you. Your instructor at the school you have been attending might be willing to act in this capacity; people with the more senior qualifications of the Association of British Riding Schools and the British Horse Society will have had both training and experience in buying horses for themselves and for clients. The most familiar qualification of a suitable standard is the full

British Horse Society Instructor certificate, which has three sections, Equitation, Teaching and Stable Manager. Anyone with the full BHSI or simply the Stable Manager's certificate is qualified in examining horses for clients, so should certainly be able to help you. Of course, there are many excellent horsemasters who have lower qualifications or none at all. This qualification is offered to you as a reliable guide.

Of course, the final decision is up to you. There is no point being pushed into buying a horse you just do not like, no matter how highly recommended he may be. However, if your adviser is definitely against a particular horse for any reason, it would seem foolish to ignore his or her opinion.

Solicitor

Few people, I feel, will consult a solicitor before buying a horse, which is a pity. Buying live animals can be fraught with difficulties, but some risk is taken out of the exercise by buying an animal with a warranty. A warranty is a guarantee that the horse is the vendor's legal property to sell, and that it complies with the description laid down in the warranty and fulfils specific conditions. All sorts of implications can be put into and left out of warranties, which is why I recommend you to discuss warranties with a solicitor. Get a copy of any warranty offered and show it to him – and, incidentally, to your horse consultant.

If your warranty describes a chestnut mare, seven years, warranted sound in traffic, to box, shoe and clip, you may think you are onto a good thing. However, you may find that you do, indeed, have a chestnut mare who is seven years old and who behaves well in some traffic (i.e. she may not object to cars or double decker buses) but bolts at the appearance of motorbikes and tractors. You may well be able to get her into a horsebox, your farrier may be able to shoe her easily and she doesn't turn a hair at being clipped, but she won't be caught out of her field. After all, she wasn't warranted sound to catch, nor was she warranted safe in *all* traffic. You could probably discuss everything you need to in half an hour with your solicitor, and the cost should not be more than a few pounds.

Vices (bad or dangerous habits or practices on the part of the horse) are things which should really be included in your warranty. The booklet recommended earlier gives a very full list and distinguishes between a vice and an unsoundness; the latter should be covered in the veterinary examination, about which more soon.

Some horses have vices which are quite tolerable to their owners. Crib-biters or cribbers are a case in point. A crib-biter seizes hold of any convenient projection (manger, top of stable door etc.), arches his neck, forms a vacuum in his throat and then sucks in a gulp of air. A wind-sucker does the same thing without getting hold of anything. Now there are many cribbers who lead active, useful lives and their owners simply ignore their pastime. Other people claim they would never have a cribber or wind-sucker in the yard because both habits cause indigestion, crib-biting damages the incisor teeth and so interferes with grazing, and both habits are catching – other horses in the yard may start doing them. In fact, these habits are by no means usually catching and not everyone agrees that they cause indigestion. The stallion of a friend of mine only started to crib-bite *after* he developed indigestion. When his diet was changed his indigestion went and so did the cribbing.

Some vices, however, such as bolting and rearing, are extremely dangerous and certainly not to be tolerated. Your adviser will discuss these matters with you, but bear in mind that your prospective purchase should be 'warranted viceless'; otherwise, any vices that you feel are tolerable should be specifically excluded from the warranty. Vices should, whatever anyone thinks, reduce the price of the horse.

It is a fact that these days many sales take place with no warranty whatsoever. Since the Trade Descriptions Act became law, giving the consumer more powers, many owners are reluctant to give warranties. Some provide a bill of sale saying that the horse is sold to Ms/Mr X as seen, tried and approved, putting the onus definitely on the buyer. So it is still very much a case of 'Let the buyer beware', hence the need for expert advice. This does not mean that if you are sold a pup and have been blatantly deceived you have no recourse, but sorting out the matter can be very expensive, uncertain and long drawn out, so it pays to be as certain as possible that the horse is what you want before signing on the dotted line or parting with your money.

Veterinary Surgeon

Once you have actually found a horse you would like (see Chapter 5) you must engage a vet to give it a thorough examination for health and soundness. This is not a legal requirement but plain common sense. Even if you don't consult any other experts, don't forego using a vet. Only a vet can medically examine the horse and uncover, maybe through X-rays or blood tests, whether it is well and sound enough for the job you require of it. You don't want a horse with such a serious heart defect that he is likely to drop down dead the first time you canter him, do you? Yet only a vet can tell you about this – unless the vendor is being particularly righteous!

Vets no longer declare a horse to be 'sound' or 'unsound' because, like humans or any other animal, many useful horses have some little thing wrong with them. These days they examine a horse and tell you whether, in their professional opinion, the horse is suitable for the job you have told them you want it to do. If you want an endurance horse or an event horse, or a horse to hunt in fast company, you will need a much sounder animal than one used for gentle hacking or dressage. So for your own sake you must be scrupulously honest with the vet about your equestrian aspirations.

All vets take the same kind of basic training, and in addition to the letters M R C V S (Member of the Royal College of Veterinary Surgeons) some have the qualifications B V Sc (Bachelor of Veterinary Science) or B VetMed (Bachelor of Veterinary Medicine). They are all, however, similarly qualified, even those with solely M R C V S after their names, who will be older members of the profession.

Some vets specialize in small animals, some in large animals, while some work in a mixed practice, and yet others deal with only one species of animal. There is no qualification enabling a vet to be a specialist in any field. If they specialize, they do so from choice.

How can you tell which vet to get to (a) look over your new horse and (b) care for it once you've got it home? If your expert horse adviser cannot recommend a suitable vet, write to the British Equine Veterinary Association for the names of members practising both in the horse's area and in your own area, if the two are not the same. They will not actually recommend anyone, but will provide you with a list of names to contact. Recommendations from other horse owners are useful, too.

The vet will charge for travelling time and mileage, and for the inspection itself (which can take an hour or so), but it is an expense you must not skimp on. You don't have to be with him or her; the vet will ring you up after the visit and tell you about the horse, and also provide a veterinary certificate describing the horse and its state of soundness.

The examination itself is most thorough. The vet will watch the horse in action to check whether he crosses his legs and is likely to bring you both down (not unknown!) or whether it moves straight and true. He or she will check his eyesight, hearing, heart and lungs, legs and feet, and may ask to take X-rays of legs and feet and a blood sample to check his state of general health and to see if the horse is on any painkilling drugs which could mask lameness.

Do not under any circumstances agree, in writing or otherwise, to buy a horse before your vet has seen it. If you must, stipulate that you will buy only subject to a successful outcome to the veterinary inspection. Otherwise you could be construed, in law, as having contracted to buy a horse whom your vet might later discover to be a dud.

Insurance Broker

There are two types of insurance which I regard as essential. The first is third party insurance to cover any damage your horse does to people and property, and the second is to cover vet's fees in the case of sickness or injury, to ensure that you can afford to give your horse the professional medical care he needs. Third party insurance, as mentioned earlier, is free to members of the British Horse Society (full details from them) and it is normally cheaper to join the BHS than to pay a premium. The BHS does excellent work, much of it unseen, to benefit the horse world and deserves your membership fee, anyway. As for the vet's fees' insurance, one company is in 1985 offering cover (after the first £25) up to £2,000 for any one injury or sickness for the nominal sum of £1 per week. Anyone who can't afford £1 a week, or is not prepared to pay it, should not be keeping a horse!

Two other kinds of insurance are personal accident for yourself, and insurance to cover the death, destruction or disability of the horse. Personal accident and sickness/permanent health plan insurances are, in my opinion, desirable but expensive and poor value for money, particularly for women who often have a premium load of 50 per cent imposed due to their assumed extra fragility and definite longer lifespans. Insurance of the horse himself is often so expensive that most people simply will not pay, particularly for an animal who is fairly valuable, as it is calculated on a percentage-of-value basis. Within three or four years you can easily pay the cost of the horse again in premiums, and I have to say, with the greatest respect, that insurance companies in general do not have a good reputation for being fair and paying up when circumstances demand. If they can possibly get out of paying up, either for death or 'loss of use' (i.e. where due to sickness or injury the horse can no longer do the job it was bought for), they do so.

I can relate many horror stories concerning people trying to get insurance companies to honour their obligations – like the case of the girl whose vet advised immediate destruction when her horse broke its shoulder in a cross-country fall, but who did not get a penny out of her insurance company; the company claimed that her policy stipulated that their own vet (from hundreds of miles away and unavailable) was the only one who could authorize destruction, notwithstanding the fact that the horse was in agony. When I attempted to claim a loss of use payment because my horse had developed a respiratory complaint, my company tried to insist that the condition should be proved by galloping the horse across country until he virtually dropped. Naturally I refused to treat my horse in such a despicable manner – and they, in turn, refused to pay out. They couldn't understand why I would not renew the policy!

In law, you are responsible for both your horse's behaviour and his welfare. This means that if he kicks someone and breaks their leg; if he gets loose and ruins a crop in the next field, or breaks down someone's fence and tramples their garden; if he bites off their car aerial (my horse did this regularly when he got the chance) or gets into their feed store and demolishes all their oats (which would probably kill him), you have to pay for the damage – and it can be very expensive.

On the other hand, if, in kicking out, he breaks his own leg (not always fatal by any means), gets severe colic from eating the growing crop, ruptures his intestine after swallowing the car aerial or makes himself seriously ill from eating the surfeit of oats, again, it is you who are responsible for putting him to rights and restoring his health. Otherwise you could be prosecuted for causing him unnecessary suffering – and both the restoration to health and the prosecution can, again, be very expensive.

Insurance to cover these two eventualities should therefore be taken out. The others are a matter of personal inclination.

Equestrian magazines usually carry advertisements from various insurance companies to which you can apply; otherwise go to a reputable broker and get them to sort out a quote for what you want. Some companies give discounts to members of various societies, such as the B H S, while others give them for horses kept on dust-free bedding (which helps maintain respiratory health) or given hay-age (see Chapter 8) to eat instead of hay, for the same reason.

The best advice regarding insurance policies is, as ever, to read the small print very carefully indeed. Always get any doubtful points clearly explained by the broker or a solicitor.

5. Now Find Your Horse

So far you will have decided what kind of horse or pony you want, and you will have thought carefully about the different systems of management and where you are going to keep him. If you have decided not to keep him at home, at least for your first year, you will have at least one address of a suitable yard where he could live, and you will also be armed with the names and addresses of various expert advisers. It is best to visit your prospective yard before looking for a horse, to make sure they are likely to have a vacancy; otherwise you could place yourself in the position of owning your dream horse without being able to provide a home for him.

Now the momentum is building up and you are actively searching for a horse of your own. There are various sources and we'll discuss them in this chapter.

Horse Dealers

Unfortunately the horse-dealing world does not have the best of reputations. This stems from the days when most dealers were shady characters (as many people feel their descendants, second-hand car salesmen, are today) only too willing to doctor up the most decrepit of equine wrecks in order to make a quick pound or two. Unfortunately, despite modern consumer laws, such characters do still exist.

Happily, however, there are reputable dealers around who understand the importance of providing their clients with an animal to suit them. The horse world is vast, but at the same time it is quite small – in other words, people who gain a bad reputation in it tend to keep it because word travels far and fast.

It is in a dealer's interests to sell you the right horse. A reputable one will put himself or herself out to fix you up and will often take back an animal which turns out – within a reasonable length of time to be mutually agreed – to be unsuitable. Also, if and when you wish to change your first horse for another, he or she will almost certainly take it back from you, not necessarily at a loss to you if you have improved the animal, and set it in part exchange against another.

How can you tell a good dealer from a bad one? Again, local or even national reputation is the best way. Your horse consultant/ adviser should know the people in your area and should also distinguish good from bad. The school you have been attending should know the various dealers, as should local horsepeople. Relationships between human beings are very personal, and anyone, dealer or client, can make a mistake, but if you keep hearing bad stories about a particular dealer, or if everyone to whom you mention a certain name gives you a cynical laugh or a knowing look, that would be good enough reason to keep away.

It may be harder to find a dealer than any other service, and in this connection you will find the *British Equestrian Directory* (see Appendix B) of great help as it lists dealers all over the country. Of course, just because they are listed does not mean they are reputable, but most of them are, and at least you have a long list of contacts to go at.

Incidentally, I feel it is false economy, despite travelling costs, to restrict your search to a small locality. Remember, you hope your horse will be with you for a long time, so you should be prepared to travel to see really promising-sounding animals and so perhaps make the right choice first time.

Auction Sales

Buying at a sale can be extremely risky, even for the knowledge-able. If you wave at a friend or even scratch your nose, you could find yourself legally obliged to buy a horse you don't want! Good sales sell warranted animals, and here the risk is reduced pro-vided you have studied the warranty thoroughly beforehand and it is acceptable to you. Other conditions than warranties may allow you to return a horse within a given time if you find, during that time, that it is unsuitable. Buying an animal 'as seen', with no warranty or guarantees of any kind, is an occupation only safe for knackermen, and it is a sad and tragic fact of life that the meat trade is where many sale animals go, despite the fact that they are young and healthy. It is hard to believe, maybe, but true.

If you still fancy buying at an auction sale, don't do so without taking along your consultant and being guided by him or her. Study the conditions of sale, which should be posted up or available from the auctioneers beforehand. You will find sales advertised in the local press and in the national equestrian press.

Breed Societies

If you want an animal of a certain breed, or a recognized partbred of that breed, contact the breed society concerned (see Appendix A), who will probably be able to give you contacts. If you buy from a breeder you will almost certainly only be able to get young stock (animals up to about three years old, or occasionally four) so you will have a very green (untrained) animal who will have to be schooled. You may be a competent rider or whip well able to school your own horse, but if you are not it is inadvisable to buy such a young animal unless you are prepared to pay to have it professionally schooled. A green horse and a less than competent rider are a disastrous combination. Emphasize to the breed society that you want a mature, trained animal so that they can give you what appropriate contacts they have.

Riding Schools

It could be an ideal arrangement for you to buy your favourite horse from the school you have been attending, if he is for sale. You will know him well, and he may recognize you out of the many scores of people he sees every week. The main thing to remember is that some school horses used to working and going out only in company become determined nappers and jibbers when taken out of their familiar environment and asked to work alone. They dig in their toes firmly and refuse to move, becoming actively difficult, bucking, kicking and maybe rearing when strong persuasion is applied. This may be just a phase which can be overcome with expert help, and it may not happen to you, but it is something to be aware of.

In fact, this business of changing environments (covered in

Chapter 8) upsets many horses, who feel like a child sent to a new school, but most of them do get over it successfully and settle down. 'Private' horses as well as school horses suffer from it, so compassion must be exercised, along with sensible firmness.

Private Sellers

Ask anyone who has a good deal of experience in buying and selling horses and you will probably be told that private sellers are the worst people to buy from. They have no professional reputation to maintain and, as they are not actually in business but selling the horse as a private citizen, they are not in the same legal position as professionals such as dealers and riding schools. If a private seller sells you an animal which he or she describes as 'sound and viceless as far as I am aware', and it turns out not to come up to that description, that little phrase 'as far as I am aware' is the vendor's get-out. It is you who have to prove that they were aware otherwise, rather than the other way round! If you have engaged a consultant who advises you to buy the horse, you could in practice sue that professional for negligence, but the legal costs and trouble involved are highly unlikely to be worth- while. Provided you are only a few hundred pounds out of pocket, put it all down to experience.

In other words, I do not recommend a first-time buyer to buy from a private seller, even on horse-professional advice. You will find many people who think that such advice is overcautious, but I'm sticking to it.

Agencies

If you look in the 'Horses for Sale' columns of the equestrian press, you will sometimes see agencies advertising a search service. You tell them what you want and they put out feelers to find it for you, normally charging the seller (not you) a commis- sion on the purchase price. I have heard many good reports from clients of such agencies. It takes a lot of the donkey work (forgive the pun) out of looking for a horse or pony, and sellers, too, find it convenient to let an agent link them up with buyers. Some agencies specialize in specific breeds, while others operate on a general basis, but it is well worthwhile contacting them with your requirements.

Magazines

As mentioned above, many local farming publications and horse journals, and most of the national horse magazines, have a 'Horses for Sale' column on which you can mark off anything which sounds promising. Then contact the advertiser for a preliminary discussion and, if all sounds well, go along with your adviser. Your adviser might well first talk to the advertiser on the telephone, as adverts are notorious for what they leave out rather than what they put in. You have to read between the lines, a skill you may not yet have acquired, and your adviser should know the right questions.

Horse Charities

Do not be surprised to see this source listed. Many horse charities and sanctuaries operate for the sole purpose of taking in and rescuing ill-treated animals, restoring them to good health and finding good homes for them on a permanent loan basis; for its security, the animal remains the property of the charity for the rest of its life.

Just because an animal has been ill-treated in the past does not mean it is ruined for ever. Many make ideal animals for a first-time owner and it is in the charity's and the animal's interests that the horse is matched up with a suitable 'owner'. Most of the people who run the charities are very experienced horsepeople who can assess animals well and know what they will and will not be suitable for. Some not considered suitable for 'homing', as it is called, will remain on the charity's premises for life and will not go out to the public if they have been physically wrecked to the extent that they cannot work, or psychologically damaged in some way. Any animal not able to lead a happy life of either kind is humanely destroyed on the charity's premises.

It is well worth contacting one of the organizations in Appendix A to see if they are looking for a good home for an animal which could do the work you want, and going along to see it. You could, however, find it a heart-rending experience when you see the atrocities committed by some so-called horsepeople on their animals – many cases are the result of sheer ignorance as much as wilful neglect or outright sadism.

Most charities require you to sign a legal document setting out certain conditions, the main ones being (a) to stress that the animal remains the legal property of the charity, (b) who may also remove it if they find it is being ill-treated or neglected in any way.

This source of finding a horse has frequently proved very satisfactory to all parties, especially in cases where capital to purchase an animal has been a problem, rather than regular income with which to keep it. It's well worth a look.

6. Your First Meeting

Going to see your *first* first horse can be quite disorientating; even the second and third are exhilarating. It's when you get to the sixth and beyond that the whole process becomes rather flat and maybe even depressing. You may well not recall anything you have read in this chapter when you make your first outing, for the simple reason that when you are confronted by the horse or pony you will be overcome by the momentousness of the occasion. However, some guidelines are called for, and something just might surface into your consciousness as you gaze at the glossy creature proffered for your approval.

And make no mistake about it, most sellers go to a good deal of trouble to prepare their horse for viewing. They naturally want him to look his best, especially if they know you are not an experienced owner. An expert can see through mud, tangled manes, chipped feet and untrimmed jawlines and assess the basic structure underneath; it is not so easy for the inexperienced, who may be influenced by first appearances, so every effort is normally made to create a good impression.

For this reason, if no other, it is only polite to ring and cancel your appointment if you cannot make it. If you get the reputation of being a time-waster, word could travel and busy professionals in particular might not be willing to bother with you. Good horses are not that hard to sell.

It is often said that you should arrive at least half an hour early so you can see if the vendor is working in the horse to loosen him up and wear off any stiffness or even lameness he might show on pulling out (coming out of the box). Quite honestly, if there is anything like this to hide – even if it is covered up during your

72

own and your vet's inspection – it will soon show itself when you get the horse home, and, if you have a warranty or a precautionary agreement to have the horse on a week's (insured) trial, you will be able to ring the seller immediately it is noticed and return the horse.

Week's trials are not uncommon, especially among good dealers, and do help you get to know the horse's nature and temperament, too, so it is advisable to arrange for one if at all possible. The insurance which will doubtless be insisted upon during this period will be at your expense, not the seller's.

A first-time owner inspecting horses is usually advised to look first at the feet and legs, for without four good feet and legs your horse will be useless. However, there is much to be said for looking first at the overall impression the horse creates, whether his make and shape appear harmonious or whether he seems awkward and as if his front half doesn't fit his back! It is impossible to acquire an eye for a horse, as it is called, without much experience, although books on conformation and anatomy can help considerably, but if you have been associating with horses regularly you will be able to form some idea of whether you like him or not on your first impression.

If the horse is in his box, the first you will see of him is his head over the door. His head and face, and particularly his eyes, can tell you a good deal about him. A kindly, interested expression is what you want for your first horse. If you are very experienced, you can probably cope with a very alert horse full of nervous energy; but even so, if the horse has a mean expression, with his ears flattened back instead of flicking forward to meet you, and maybe his nostrils wrinkled up and back, it indicates that he is not pleased to meet you – not a very good start.

Your adviser will probably conduct the examination for the most part, and it will probably run something like this. You should be taken to the horse's box (unless you are seeing him in his field) and he will be brought out for you. Have a look inside the box and see if the bedding is disarranged or the walls are badly scuffed, kicked or chewed. If they are, ask if it is his normal box and make a note that the animal showed signs of restless behaviour – not a sign of a calm temperament – and discuss it afterwards with your adviser.

The horse will be stripped (rugs removed, if worn) and stood up (posed) for you to look at. At this stage, you will not really know what you are looking for unless you have made a study of conformation, but your adviser will. Basically, he or she will

73

probably first stand back to get an overall picture of the horse, both sides, front and back, looking for balanced make and shape and whether the horse has four straight legs, one at each corner.

This may sound funny, but to a knowledgeable horsemaster it describes probably the most important conformational quality to look for. When looked at from in front, a leg is described as 'straight' if a line can be dropped perpendicularly to the ground from the point of the shoulder, through the centre of the knee, straight down the centre front of the cannon bone, through the centre of the fetlock and down the very front of the hoof to the toe. Looking at a back leg, such a line should be able to be dropped from the point of the buttock, through the hock, down the back of the leg, through the centre of the fetlock and down between the heels to the ground. This leg conformation is very important if you want a horse whose legs will bear stresses and forces evenly. Uneven stresses precipitate lameness, and a lame horse cannot be used. There are enough things to lame a horse in this world without adding faulty conformation.

To check if the hooves are balanced, when looking from the front the 'ends' of the coronet band (from which the hoof horn grows down) should each be the same height from the ground, and this should apply to each hoof. When looking from the side, the angle with the ground produced by the front of the hoof wall should form a continuous line with the front of the pastern immediately above it, allowing for a very slight 'bump' for the coronet itself. If the coronet appears to drop, however, so that the slope of the pastern is steeper (more upright) than that of the hoof, or if it appears to protrude upwards so that the pastern is less steep (nearer the horizontal) than the hoof wall, this indicates lack of balance. The condition may be due to faulty trimming by the farrier or poor conformation of the horse, but it is a matter to discuss with your adviser. As mentioned earlier, other points of conformation can be studied in one of the books recommended in Appendix B.

When your adviser has seen the horse stood up, he or she will ask for it to be led away at a walk and returned at a trot. The animal's action will be watched from sides, front and back to see if he moves his legs straight forward and back without deviating in sideways (in or out) movements. A horse that brings his legs in during movement to the extent that he kicks himself (known as brushing if low down, speedicutting if high up) will have to wear protective boots during work and could even bring himself down in extreme circumstances.

74

The movement is checked from the side to see if the horse 'overtracks' when walking and 'tracks up' when trotting, i.e. puts his hind feet down in front of the 'print' left by the forefeet when walking, or on the same spot when trotting. This trotting up and walking when led in hand should be carried out on hard, level ground such as a strip of concrete, so that the action can be accurately observed. Hardness brings out any slight unevenness in gait or lameness, whereas soft ground disguises it, and sloping ground makes it less easy to assess action and stance properly.

Your adviser will probably run his or her hands down the legs, feeling for lumps and bumps which cannot be seen but which could indicate wear and tear and possible future lameness, and will pick up the feet to see if they are well conformed and healthy underneath. He will probably also look at the teeth, to check age and, possibly, uneven wear of the front teeth which could indicate that the horse is a crib-biter, and will generally run his hands over the horse to see if he objects to being handled, and to assess the condition of the skin, which should be elastic and pliable, and the coat smooth and glossy.

Note all the time the horse's reaction to people around it. He should accept people's attentions with equanimity and should appear well behaved and interested (maybe especially in pockets which have been known to contain tit-bits!) in what is going on.

If the horse was in a field when you arrived, note whether he was easy to catch. Nothing is more infuriating, and, indeed, useless, than a horse who won't be caught – and it is a failing which is extremely difficult to cure.

After this initial inspection the horse can be ridden or driven. You should first see the owners or staff ride him, as you want to see how he normally behaves in familiar surroundings. Remember, if at a dealer's, that the surroundings may, in fact, not be familiar to the horse unless he has been there some time.

Note whether or not he objects to being tacked or harnessed up and whether he stands to be mounted or fidgets about. If you are reasonably experienced, you will be able to tell how he is going in work. Is the horse reluctant to accept the bit, with head high and an uncooperative or anxious expression on his face (this could be his human partner's fault, of course) or does he 'bridle' nicely, not excessively champing the bit or bringing his chin in towards his chest so that the front line of his face slopes down and back (known as overbending)?

Does he move as well in work as he did in hand? Does he thrash his tail about (a sign of distress or annoyance which could, again, be the result of human error) or does it swing easily from side to side as he moves? If in harness, does he manoeuvre his vehicle willingly and easily, or with difficulty and reluctance? When ridden, does he approach his jumps with confidence and calmness, or does he rush at them or even refuse?

These are all points to watch for, and your adviser should know, even if you don't, whether he is going well under saddle or whether, if not, it is his rider who is at fault.

Your adviser may well try the horse next, to see how he goes for a stranger, and then it will be your turn.

Relax and ride at your best. Be fair to the horse, who has never seen you before in his life, and simply try to assess whether you feel right and comfortable on him, whether he gives you a comfortable feel and goes willingly for you, and whether you feel you could ever make a partnership. It is true that a good deal of extra-sensory perception exists between a horse and owner who are used to each other, but even strangers can hit it off, or otherwise, at their first meeting.

If you are buying a pony for your child, the same things apply, but it is often difficult to get a child to give a true opinion – they usually say 'yes' unless they actively dislike the pony! Study them as a pair and do not be afraid to ask your adviser in front of the seller whether he or she thinks the child and pony are suited to each other.

You should, in front of your adviser, ask if the animal has any quirks of behaviour which are not necessarily vices but which should be known about, especially if it is a child's pony (for instance, does it make a mad grab at the bucket as soon as one walks in with feed – quite off-putting for a child or a novice), because you have an expert witness to the reply. However the reply can always be qualified with 'not as far as I know', which, as stated earlier, leaves you to prove otherwise.

Do ask about a week's trial if you are seriously interested, and work out details concerning insurance and transport. Technically, if the horse is being sent at your request, you could be liable for its welfare and any costs involved from the instant it leaves the seller's yard, so you must be quite clear about these matters.

Assuming you want the horse, now is the time to arrange for the veterinary examination. It is not normally advisable to expect the seller's vet to do it, as he will then be working for you rather than his normal client and may feel awkward about it, if he agrees at all. You will, however, probably already have chosen a vet to see the horse (as discussed in Chapter 4), so simply say you will get the vet to telephone and make a mutually convenient appointment.

If you say, now, that you will buy the horse, this could well be taken as a verbal contract (just as binding as a written one, especially if witnesses are there to prove it), so qualify your assent by adding 'subject to the vet's inspection', usually described as 'if he passes the vet'. Do not say you would like him if it's not true. Simply say, 'He's nice, but I don't feel he is quite what I am looking for.' If he's the best you've seen so far, but you have to visit others which might turn out just as well or better, say something like: 'I do like him very much and am definitely interested, but there are two more I have to see next week, so I can let you know then.'

The seller might then say: 'Ah, well, I have another client coming to see this horse tomorrow, and he might go.' If you feel you are being put on the spot, your adviser should now take over, if he hasn't already, as he is, or should be, used to such situations. Whatever happens, do not be pushed into buying the horse. If you are inexperienced, your adviser should negotiate, and should tactfully arrange for the horse's present owner to ring you at once should a firm offer be received, so as to give you first refusal. Then you will simply have to make up your mind whether you want him or wish to take a chance on finding something else.

A final point – remember that no horse is perfect. They all have something wrong with them, or at least imperfections if not exactly faults, and you usually get what you pay for. What you want is a horse who will do what you want, whom you like and who seems to like you, and is priced fairly.

7. Tack, Harness, Clothing and Equipment

The financial aspect of equipping your horse with tack, harness and other necessities has already been mentioned, so you will realize that it is a major item of expense which can cost you as much as the horse himself. All sorts of paraphernalia exists for horse enthusiasts, and much of it you can do without; on the other hand, there is virtually no end to what you can spend if you are so inclined. Most of us, however, need to watch our budgets, so this chapter will describe briefly what you will need, as well as what would be helpful but isn't really essential.

Buying Secondhand: Some Warnings

Setting up in horse ownership can be very expensive, so you might consider buying good-quality secondhand tack or harness. Many saddlers have a selection of used gear. Look for supple leather, not stiff as a board, with a sheen to it and which, when bent and manipulated, does not show cracks, large or small, which could break and cause an accident; for the same reason the stitching should be intact.

The most serious fault in a secondhand saddle is a broken tree (frame). You can detect this by holding the saddle firmly at front and back and trying to twist it across the seat. The saddle should not move at all, but if it does, and particularly if you can hear a grinding noise, you can be sure there is a fault in the tree. Once a tree is broken there is no point in having it mended, as there are plenty of sound, used saddles available, probably for what it
78

would cost to have the repair done. A broken-treed saddle must never be used on a horse as it can cause a serious back injury.

Where to Buy

Until you are more experienced, I recommend that you buy your equipment, new or used, only from a saddler who is a member of the Society of Master Saddlers; then you can be sure of good-quality equipment, with a qualified person available to offer reliable advice. Such a firm will also be able to offer a good after-sales service for repairs and maintenance. Saddles, for instance, need checking very frequently to make sure the stuffing has not impacted or 'settled', which will affect the fit of the saddle (see p. 80); side-saddles especially need restuffing on the side to which the legs go.

There is a good deal of foreign tack on the market, some of it very good (usually European and, occasionally, American) and some of it very poor (usually Asian). It is as well to remember that English tack and harness are among the best in the world and are normally cheaper than European and American equipment, so why not buy British? All good tack made by a member of the Society of Master Saddlers will usually be stamped 'Made in Britain' and bear the Society's distinctive oval crest, which will probably also be displayed on member saddlers' premises and on their letterheading and brochures.

Saddle and accessories: astride

Your most expensive single item will be your saddle, so choose it carefully. You will already have some experience of the various types of saddles if you have been riding regularly, and may know what you want. If not, a suitable one for all general riding from flat work to jumping is the type known as the *general-purpose saddle*. This has a moderately forward-cut flap, on which your legs rest, with knee rolls on the panel underneath for added security and comfort. Modern examples have a reasonably deep seat with the deepest point in the centre for good balance, and the most comfortable have a spring tree as opposed to a rigid tree. This means that the tree has metal strips on each side from front to back, with enough spring in them to help absorb your and the horse's movements and prevent sore bottoms and backs. That's

79

the general idea, but a poor, unbalanced, unsteady rider will give himself a sore bottom and his horse a sore back no matter what saddle he uses! (See illustration.)

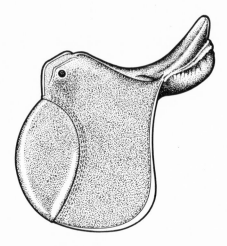

A general-purpose saddle. The seat is deep and comfortable and the flap is cut sufficiently far forward to permit jumping while not being so exaggerated that flat work is uncomfortable. These saddles are ideal for ordinary riding and cross-country. The knee rolls provide 'anchorage' for the knees when jumping

As for fit, the main point to watch for is that, when the horse's heaviest rider is in the saddle, no part of the saddle should touch the horse's spine or withers. You must be able to see a clear tunnel of daylight down the horse's back when he is mounted and should be able to fit four fingers' upright width between the front arch (pommel) of the saddle and the withers.

The saddle should not be so narrow that it pinches the sides of the withers, nor so wide that it rocks from side to side. Nor should it impede the action of the shoulder blades at the top. If the saddle is too long it will press on the horse's loins.

Your adviser will be able to help you on tack fitting, but you might also like to study this important subject, and learn about the vast array of equipment available, by referring to one of the books mentioned in Appendix B.

You will need *stirrup leathers* (unbreakable rawhide are my favourites) and *stirrups* (stainless steel for strength, not nickel)

which should be an inch wider than the widest part of your riding boot, and a *girth* to keep the saddle on. If your saddle has long girth straps, as dressage saddles and some general-purpose saddles do, you will need a short belly girth (which does away with an uncomfortable lump under your leg); otherwise a normal one will be needed. They come in various sizes, so tell the saddler the size of your horse and he will help you choose the right one. Good materials for girths are leather (if kept immaculately clean and soft), mohair and lampwick. These latter two are soft, natural, absorbent fabrics which help avoid girth galls. String, nylon and some other synthetic girths can cause friction and galling.

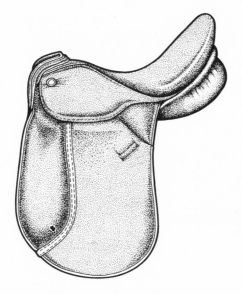

This dressage saddle should provide the ultimate in comfort. The deep seat and deeply-gusseted panel underneath it make for comfort and stability on the horse's back, while the straighter-cut flap is commensurate with the longer stirrup used for dressage. The padding provides extra comfort for knee and thigh. Although designed for specialist dressage, these saddles are being used increasingly for showing as they show off the horse's shoulder and give the judge a much more comfortable ride than traditional showing saddles – a factor which must influence him or her somewhat! People with shortish legs find these saddles equally good for jumping; my own was used for both flat work and cross-country for many years.

81

A *numnah* (saddle pad) is not essential, but can help absorb sweat and keep the saddle cleaner. If you choose a thin, quilted cotton one it will not significantly affect the fit of the saddle, but a thicker, fleecy one (either Acrilan or real sheepskin) will take up room, and although these do undoubtedly offer the horse greater comfort you must allow for their thickness when fitting your saddle.

Side-saddles and accessories

Unfortunately, side-saddles are rather more expensive than astride ones, and most of those available are secondhand, although new ones are not now so difficult to obtain since the fairly recent revival of this genre of riding. Most of them are made for the rider to sit with her (or his) legs on the near (left) side, but offside saddles are also available – however they are rare, and often have to be made to order. The Side Saddle Association (see Appendix A) will be able to help you with detailed information on make, use and fitting. Briefly, the side-saddle, like its astride counterpart, must not press on the spine or withers or bang about or press on the loins. A horse needs well-defined withers to carry a side-saddle properly; animals with low withers and/or 'loaded' shoulders (i.e. shoulders which are squarish or wide at the top, due either to fat or to conformation) do not hold a side-saddle in place well.

The saddle will have two pommels. The top one is fixed to the tree of the saddle itself but the lower one is normally adjustable. The saddle must fit the rider well, the size being taken from the measurement from behind the rider's knee to the back of the seat. There must be only a couple of inches of space behind the rider's seat. The saddle seat (usually doeskin, which is less slippery than ordinary leather) must be quite straight and flat from front to back and side to side, because it is extremely difficult to sit properly, and to rise at the trot, in a saddle which dips, as some do with age or simply from bad design.

The saddle will have full flaps on both sides, but under the flap, at the front, is a point strap to which the front girth buckle should be fastened. The strap is angled backwards at 15 degrees to assist positioning and security. The remaining girth buckle is fastened usually to the front girth strap.

In addition to the *girth* there is a *belly strap* which goes over the girth, and a diagonal *balance strap* on the side away from the
82

A cob mare of the type recommended for all-round family use, suitable for adults and older children. Study her 'chunky' conformation, typical of cobs. Her legs, however, are not coarse and heavy and she is altogether a very useful type of animal for a first-time owner. She is wearing an eggbutt snaffle bridle with a correctly fitted drop noseband, together with a general-purpose saddle

A 16-hands high ex-racehorse Thoroughbred gelding of an ideal type and scope for general riding club and local show work. He has a particularly kind temperament and an ever-youthful outlook, despite being sixteen years old, and belies the general belief that ex-racehorses are hot-headed and only suitable for experts. The style of clip he has been given is known as the Irish clip

A champion working hunter coping perfectly with the brush hurdle type of jump usually presented in such classes, along with the rustic (i.e. not painted) poles, all of which are intended to give a 'natural' impression to simulate the hunting field. The jumps are not high, but are designed to show the horse's style and willingness to go confidently at his fences

A lovely Arab-cross mare, here correctly turned out (in plaits and double bridle) for an in-hand broodmare class. Animals of her type can be used in many types of classes, but particularly Arab breed classes and hack classes. She is not at all of suitable type for show hunter classes

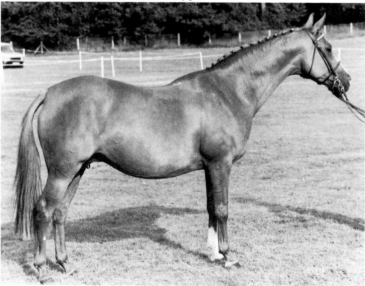

(left) This Welsh-type pony is obviously making its rider very happpy. Native ponies like this are excellent all-round children's ponies and it is essential that they instill confidence into their small charges, which this one clearly does

(right) A lovely little Exmoor pony, ideal for its young rider. The pony's expression – showing kindness, intelligence and alert interest – is what should be looked for in any animal

An excellent all-round family pony, suitable for all but the smallest children and the heavier adults. At 14.3 hands high, he has strength and substance without courseness. This particular pony has a most generous nature and is a willing, active worker. His facial expression reveals his calm, friendly nature. His clip is a trace clip

This is a lovely 14.2 hands high New Forest pony, and he is carrying his adult rider very well side-saddle

This cob-type family all-rounder is here showing his versatility in harness. The first-time owner could move on from an animal like this to a larger or more Thoroughbred type and put the first horse to driving. This would be particularly appropriate for a pony

rider's legs, going from the girth to near the back of the saddle to help prevent its rocking and giving the horse a sore back.

It is essential to use a side-saddle which has a *quick-release device* at the top of the stirrup leather. They don't all, so do check without fail – if you fall off or get unseated, particularly to the side opposite the one where your legs are, and you get your foot caught in the stirrup, you could get dragged, seriously injured and maybe killed. It is true that if your stirrup is, as recommended earlier, neither more nor less than 1 inch wider than the widest part of the sole of your boot, it is very unlikely that your foot will get caught – but you never know, and cannot take too many precautions on this score. If your stirrup is more than 1 inch wider than your boot, your foot could slip through and get caught by the heel. If it is narrower than this, your boot could jam in the stirrup with equally serious results. *Safety stirrups* themselves are available and, if used in conjunction with a device which will release the leather itself in an emergency, should virtually guarantee your safety in this respect in the event of your parting company with your horse.

There should be a *hook* on the bottom of the stirrup leather, too, which passes through the eye at the top of the iron and back on itself, adjusting onto the holes in the leather itself. Side-saddle stirrups have extra-large eyes to take the hook, and the leathers, too, are of a slightly different design from astride equipment.

Bridle, bit and reins

You will obviously need a bridle and bit, and will probably start off with a *snaffle*, using whatever bit suits your new horse as advised by his former owner and your adviser. A snaffle bridle will also take a *pelham* bit (see below) instead of a snaffle, if required, and whatever the purists and many instructors say, many horses go very kindly in a pelham provided the rider has good hands. (See illustrations.)

Most snaffle bits comprise a single mouthpiece, sometimes 'broken' (jointed) and sometimes in a half-moon shape. You can also get straight-bar snaffles, but most horses dislike them as they squash the tongue. The mouthpiece can be joined to the rings at each end by an extension of itself up and down the rings for a short way (called an eggbutt), or simply have holes through each end of the mouthpiece through which the snaffle rings pass. Eggbutts do prevent the corners of the horse's mouth being

83

pinched between the mouthpiece and the ring, which is extremely painful, but some horses prefer the looser action of the loose-ring or wire-ring snaffle.

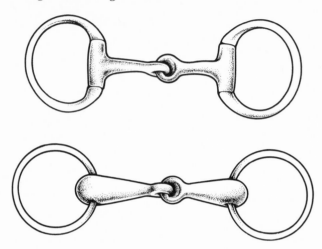

Two kinds of snaffle bit. An ordinary eggbut (top) and a German (thicker mouth) wire ring snaffle. Both eggbut and wire ring or loose ring bits are available with rubber-covered mouthpieces for a softer feel in the mouth

There are many other sorts of snaffle, about which you can learn from your instructor or adviser or from a good saddlery book. Whatever kind you buy, always ask for stainless steel, as with stirrups, as it is much stronger than nickel. If you require a rubber-covered mouthpiece, you may have to settle for nickel as they are rare in stainless steel.

Pelham bits are an attempt to give the rider the effect of a double bridle (with snaffle reins attached at the mouthpiece and curb reins attached at the bottom of the cheekpiece, giving, by means of a curb chain in the horse's chin groove, the flexing leverage of the curb) without the horse's having two bits in his mouth. Many experts say pelhams fail to do either job but, as mentioned above, many horses go happily in them. (See illustration.)

Bitting is a vast subject on which you may well need the help of your instructor or adviser. The important thing to remember is that, whatever bit is used, a great deal depends on the sensitivity and skill of the hands at the other end of the reins.

Your reins must be comfortable to hold, otherwise it will affect

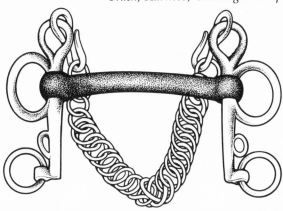

This is a short-cheeked vulcanite, half-moon (sometimes called 'mullen-mouthed') pelham bit with chain. Many horses go kindly in these bits, particularly those horses who dislike jointed mouthpiece snaffles. The chain is not necessary, a leather curb strap being quite sufficient, and kind if kept well cleaned and soft

your handling of them. This, in turn, adversely affects the feel you get of the horse's mouth and the feel he has *in* his mouth.

Reins come in varying types and lengths. Showjumping and pony reins are the shortest and driving reins, obviously, the longest. Tell your saddler the size of your animal and what you want the reins for and he should be able to fix you up with the correct length.

As for width, there is a mania in some quarters for super-fine reins, usually for showing ponies and hacks. However, too-narrow reins for the size of your hands can tend to make you clench the reins and become 'mutton-fisted', lacking sensitivity and finesse in their handling. On the other hand, wide ones are difficult to hold and manipulate and do not make for relaxation and a kind 'feel' on the horse's mouth.

The only way you can find out what is right for you is to try different widths. As a suggestion, most women are comfortable with ⅞-inch reins and most men with ¾ inch. Small children often like ½-inch reins and, as a matter of interest, on double bridles and pelhams the curb rein is often of this width, with the top (bridoon or snaffle) rein a size wider.

The simplest reins are of plain leather, but these give no hold at all when wet from rain or sweat, even if you wear gloves. Some plain leather reins have little strips of leather laced through them in a herringbone pattern (called 'laced reins') which is a help. Other reins are of 5-strand plaited leather and, although they give a good hold, they do stretch with use. Plaited reins also come in nylon (rather rough on the hands and, again, prone to stretching) and heavy cotton, which are comfortable (if kept washed) and do not seem to stretch unreasonably.

My own favourites for general riding are rubber-covered leather. The rubber has tiny, flat pimples to provide hold, and the best of this type of rein have the rubber stitched on by a single row of stitching down the middle. The stitching inevitably weakens the leather, so should not be small. The type with two rows of stitching has obviously been weakened further. The rubber does wear with use, but can normally be replaced once, after which the reins will have to be thrown away as they will be too weak for safety after a third row of stitching has been put in.

Reins normally come in pairs, buckling together at the top (hand) end and fastening to the bit rings at the other with various types of fastenings, the most common being called 'hook studs', where a small metal hook is set near the end of the rein, a continuing flap of leather passed through the bit ring and the hook pressed through a specially-sized hole in the flap. Always make sure the flap is tucked in its little keeper (loop) on the rein for neatness and security.

Driving harness

There is quite a variety of harness to choose from and, if you have been driving for some time, you may well know just what you want. If you intend to drive just for non-competitive fun, you can get away with much cheaper harness than if you are showing. You can, for instance, buy synthetic harness which is strong and easy to care for, if not smart. Whether showing or not, you can use *breast harness*, in which case the horse takes the traction on his breast and the fronts (above the points) of his shoulders, instead of buying a much more expensive *collar*. Breast harness is used extensively in competitive carriage driving as it is lighter than a collar, but because of the comparatively small weight-bearing area it is only suitable if the horse's load is light.

A collar puts the load evenly around the horse's shoulders and makes pulling a heavy load easier for him. Collars are also considered much smarter than breast harness for showing. The collar should lie flat on the shoulders and you should be able to fit two fingers between the collar and the neck, and your hand between the windpipe and the bottom of the collar. The collar must bear evenly when the horse is working – if it is uneven or unsteady, the pressure and friction could cause sore shoulders. Just as saddles need periodic checking and possible restuffing, so driving collars have to be watched and checked, more because of the horse or pony's differing muscular development, which varies with work – the more muscled up the animal, the larger the collar he will need, so you may need more than one.

You will also need a *driving pad* and *saddle* which, like a riding saddle, must be clear of the spine, plus *girth* and, over the top of the pad and girth, a *belly band* with tugs to take the shafts and a *back band*. The *back strap* runs from this section of the harness along the spine, and the *crupper* is fastened to it. The horse's tail must fit comfortably in the crupper, which must be kept very clean and well oiled, and it should be fitted just tight enough to stop the pad riding forward. Any tighter, and it will cause soreness; any looser, and it will be useless.

A *breeching* and a *loin strap*, if used, will be more expensive, but they do help the horse in slowing down and stopping. Despite this, many competitive cross-country driving teams do not have them, as it is one more item to catch on tree branches and so on in the rough and tumble of this event.

The breeching, if used, should lie about 12 inches below the root of the tail, and just touch the buttocks when the horse is standing. The loin strap will be vertical, slanting forward slightly when the breeching is being used in slowing down or stopping.

You will also obviously need a pair of *traces* which hook to the collar at the front and to the vehicle at the back, preferably by means of a *swingle tree* (a movable horizontal bar chained to the vehicle) or a spring hook attachment. These absorb the movements of the vehicle and help avoid sore shoulders.

Your driving *bridle* will be similar to a riding bridle but more substantial, often with metal *rosettes* at the base of the ears and a decorative brass *browband*. The *blinkers* (or winkers) are fitted in such a way that the horse's eyes are behind the centre of them and their widest part is at the same height as the horse's eye. They must not chafe or press on or around the eyes in any way. You will need a pair of *driving reins* and finally a *bit*.

Some horses are driven in a *Wilson (or double-ring) snaffle* with a jointed mouthpiece. This can be very severe, as can all jointed mouthpieces, because of the so-called nutcracker or squeezing action of the V-shaped mouthpiece if the reins are pulled hard.

Remember that just as delicate a touch is required for a driving horse as for a riding horse; good hands are essential. The cheekpieces of the bridle are fastened to the floating rings of the Wilson snaffle and the reins around not just one but both rings, to avoid excessively severe action. (See illustration.)

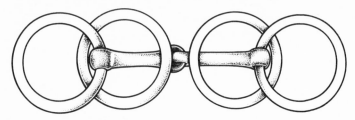

A Wilson driving snaffle. The inner rings are fastened to the bridle cheek pieces and the outer ones to the reins

The *Liverpool driving bit* has a straight mouthpiece – which should always be used smooth side to the horse's tongue because the other, grooved, side is severe – with a short lower cheek to provide alternative rein positions, and is used with a curb chain.

A bit which most horses find more comfortable because of the extra room allowed for the tongue is the *Elbow or Army Universal*. This has a port (arch) in the mouthpiece for the tongue, is used with a curb chain and also provides alternative rein positions.

The fit of any bridle is important. If it causes discomfort the horse could start tossing and shaking his head, making cooperation unlikely and control difficult, not to mention making the horse unhappy.

Starting at the top, the *browband* should be of such a size that it holds the headpiece comfortably behind the horse's ears without pulling it into the base of them, as it will if it is too small. On the other hand, if it is too big it might flop about and irritate the horse, and the bridle will be insecure.

If you use a *cavesson noseband*, which is just a loop round the nose supported by a leather strap passing over the poll, it should lie midway between the horse's sharp cheekbones and the corners of his mouth, and you should be able to fit two fingers' width between it and the front of the nose. (These nosebands serve no useful purpose unless your horse needs head control by means of a standing martingale – and the point of these is a matter on which even experts disagree. A first horse, however, should not need one.)

The second most popular type of noseband is the *drop noseband*. Here, the back straps drop below the bit into the chin groove, making it difficult for the horse to evade the bit by opening his mouth. The front strap should be fitted well above the nostrils, only slightly below where you would fit a cavesson, otherwise the horse's breathing will be severely restricted. Horses cannot breathe through their mouths, and free passage for air intake is essential. It is, therefore, quite wrong to fit a drop noseband, as is often seen, with the front strap down near the nostrils.

The *throatlatch* (pronounced throatlash) fastens under the throat and you should be able to fit the width of four fingers between it and the horse's round jawbones. This should keep the bridle secure but not restrict breathing.

Your *reins* must be comfortable to hold, otherwise your handling of them will be affected and so will the resulting feel of (and in) the horse's mouth. There are many varieties, though all driving reins are usually plain.

Driving vehicles

A discussion of the various types of vehicles is outside the scope of this book. Whatever you choose, however, it should suit your horse or pony in type and should be neither too big and heavy nor too small and light for him. When put to (in the shafts), your horse must not live in fear of catching his legs on the vehicle, which would quickly ruin him as a driving horse. The vehicle should stay clear enough of his tail to prevent any chance of contact, so the shafts should be of a suitable length to ensure this. The points of the shafts should be just behind the fronts of his shoulders, and the shafts themselves must not be too narrow or they could rub his sides and make him sore.

In tacking up or harnessing, always remember that any undue pressure or friction can cause rubbing, which will eventually lead to soreness. This creates an unhappy and maybe fractious horse who is neither a pleasure to drive, nor safe.

Rugs

You are almost certain to need a rug for your horse in winter, unless he is the type who grows a thick coat. Even if he does, if you want to work him at anything more than a walk and short trot you will need to clip his coat to prevent excessive sweating (which can cause loss of condition and a tendency to get chills); a rug is then needed to compensate for the loss of his natural insulation.

Various rugs are available made from lightweight synthetic fabrics which are easy to launder and dry. You can choose from quilted nylon, usually with a brushed cotton lining for comfort and non-slip qualities, the type filled with polyester beads (you need a large-capacity washing machine for these), and those made from such fabrics as Equitex and Thermatextron, which work on the principle of allowing body moisture to escape while being showerproof, too.

There is no need, these days, to buy a rug which has to be kept on by means of a *surcingle* (belt) round the horse's middle. These are neither the most comfortable for the horse nor the most

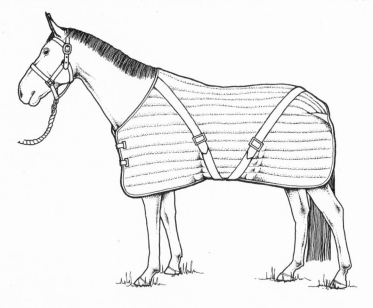

A well-fitting rug. It comes right back to the root of the tail and well forward in front of the withers, not pressing on top of them. It is deep enough for warmth and roomy enough for comfort. This method of fastening, with crossed surcingles attached to the rug, is another excellent method, in addition to those mentioned in the text, as it causes no pressure on the back. This rug is shaped to follow the outline of the horse's spine and is darted at the back for a cosy fit

secure. Sometimes surcingles are stitched to rugs and cause considerable pressure on the spine, often resulting in soreness. If a separate surcingle is used, padding such as a folded piece of blanket can be put between it and the rug to reduce the pressure, but this is not entirely satisfactory.

Proper *rollers* (wide surcingles with built-in padding which goes on each side of the spine) are much better as they virtually remove pressure, but they still have to be buckled on and, like surcingles, when the horse lies down his abdomen expands and he will undoubtedly be able to feel the roller.

A much more comfortable arrangement for the horse is the modern type of rug which is kept on by means of narrow surcingles criss-crossing under his belly and attaching to the rug at shoulders and hips. These rugs are shaped to fit the horse's body and therefore naturally hang correctly and are more or less self-adjusting, returning to the correct position when the horse shakes himself after getting up. I strongly recommend them to readers; various makes can be obtained from good saddlers.

The only problem arises when the horse is clipped and needs a blanket as well as a rug. Blankets can only be kept on under a rug by means of a roller or (failing all else) a surcingle, unless you put on two rugs at once, as many owners do. Some firms make clip-in *under-rugs* for this purpose, however.

Your horse will be wearing his rug much longer than he wears his harness or saddle, and will therefore be subject to any discomfort and annoyance that it causes for that much longer. A considerable pull can be exerted on the horse when an ill-fitting rug slips round or is pulled round when the horse lies down or rolls in his stable, particularly if it is held out of place by a surcingle or roller; if the rug is on the withers, as it usually is, it can badly bruise them which may in extreme cases prevent the horse being worked.

A rug should come in front of the withers for at least a couple of inches, not on top of them as is usually seen, and should extend back to the root of the tail, not finish halfway along his quarters. The front must be roomy enough to fasten closely and keep the rug forward, but should not be tight. You should be able to pass your hand round the neck and over the withers – where you should automatically straighten out any mane hair – quite easily.

Depthwise, the rug should come down to the horse's elbows and stifles. The best rugs, which are not necessarily the most expensive, are shaped along the back seam to follow the shape of

91

the horse's back, with a rise in front for the withers, a dip for the back, another rise for the croup and another slight dip towards the root of the tail. There are plenty of good rugs shaped like this, also many with darting at elbows and hips to take up any slack fabric here, so there is no need to be pushed into buying an inferior one which because of its lack of styling will inevitably exert uneven pressure. Never buy a rug which is cut simply in a straight line along the back (spine) seam. (See illustration.)

This shaping and darting is especially important in *New Zealand (waterproof) rugs*. You may not need one of these, and they can be quite expensive, but they are an absolute boon to working owners who have to leave their horse in the field all day while they are at work. They are also invaluable for putting on a clipped horse so that he can be turned in the paddock to stretch his legs rather than remaining stabled.

New Zealand rugs can be bought with surcingles, but obviously I do not recommend this sort. The properly shaped ones are the only ones really worth considering. Most types are kept on by means of leg straps attaching at the back and halfway along inside the rug, a few inches up from the bottom edge. To prevent them rubbing the horse's skin inside his hindlegs, they should be fastened as shown in the accompanying drawing, linked through each other, as this holds them apart.

New Zealand rugs fit a little more roomily than stable rugs, particularly at the back where they should come a few inches past the root of the tail. Traditional ones are made of waxed canvas half-lined with wool for warmth; they are rather heavy but last for many years. Synthetic ones, which are also now available, are much lighter. New Zealand rugs can easily be reproofed with tent reproofer from any camping shop, or with rug reproofer which is sold by some saddlers.

General equipment

You will need a *headcollar* or *halter* in which to lead your horse and tie him up occasionally, perhaps in the yard on a nice day while you groom him, or for shoeing. You cannot use your bridle for this. Rope halters are cheap and quite useful. The headpiece and noseband are made of wide webbing and the piece behind the jaw is rope. When putting it on you should tie a knot in the rope as it goes through the bound hole on the nearside (see illustration), otherwise it will tighten if pulled on and begin to hurt the

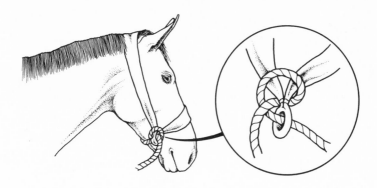

A correctly fitting webbing halter. It is essential that the knot be secured round the bound loop as shown, otherwise the halter will pull tight should the horse play up and thereby make matters worse

horse – and a horse in pain usually reacts violently, especially if his breathing is being cut off as well!

Generally, despite the slight extra expense, a proper headcollar is preferable to a halter. This is like a strong bridle with the noseband all in one, and with no bit. The best have a browband as well, for security. Serviceable ones are made of strong, washable nylon webbing but various types of leather ones are available, too. The best are adjustable on the nose as well as on the cheekpiece. The noseband, as with a bridle, should come below the sharp cheekbones, and you should be able to fit three fingers' width in it. If it is much looser it can catch on things and can be rubbed off down the nose by a crafty horse.

You will need a lead rope a good 4 feet long; the type which clips to the bottom ring on the headcollar under the lower jaw with a doglead type of clip is the most useful. Tie a knot on the other end to prevent it being pulled through your hand.

Many experienced horsemasters use a 6-foot-long rope and thread one end through the ring to form a loop, holding both loose ends in the hand, thus avoiding knots. Then if the horse breaks away – it can happen – the rope will pull itself free through the ring and the horse will not bring himself down if he treads on it and the rope jerks on the headcollar.

Incidentally, if a horse is led on a public road he should always be led in a bridle with bit for extra control.

You will probably be able to do without *bandages*, although

93

long, woollen stable bandages, used over Gamgee tissue padding, are useful if you need to dry off your horse's legs in winter. They also add warmth (equivalent to another blanket, people say) if it is very cold or he is ill.

Bandages for work are usually made of crepe or some other stretchy fabric, and you need to be really competent at using them if you do not want to lame your horse, either through overtight, uneven pressure or through the bandage coming off and tripping him. Some people maintain that bandages help to support the tendons, but all they do in practice is minimize jar a little during work. They must always be put on over padding, which can also help lessen the effect of any knocks to the cannons during jumping.

If active work is undertaken and your horse's action is slightly suspect, *brushing or speedicut boots*, which buckle on on the outside of the leg, can be bought in case he kicks himself. *Over-reach boots* (like rubber bells) can be used on the front feet of horses who tread on their own heels.

If you do not have a manger in your stable, you will doubtless find a *bucket* useful for your horse to eat from, and you will in any case need one in which to mix his feeds. An excellent range of buckets, large feed containers and muck skips is currently on the market: they are called the Kanguro unbustable range, which is virtually what they are (see Appendix A). They are made from soft but hard-wearing rubber material reinforced with vulcanized fibre. If the horse sits or stamps on them (a favourite pastime) they simply squash and spring back into shape, whereas metal or rigid plastic or polythene ones would crack and be ruined, and maybe injure the horse too.

If your stable has no hayrack, you may wish to buy a *haynet*, which is a most convenient way of feeding hay. This is just like a giant tennis-ball net which ties up at horse's head height to a ring or strong bracket on the wall. Do not let it dangle from a beam in the middle of the roof because the horse needs to press it against the wall to get hold of the hay with his teeth. (See illustration.)

Nets must never be tied lower than the horse's head, because as the horse empties them they hang lower and lower and he could then get his feet caught in them, with disastrous results if he paws when feeding or throws his legs around in ecstasy while rolling. They should be tied by passing the cord through one of the meshes, forming a half bow, then passing the loose end through the loop of the bow and giving a final pull to secure. It is

94

very difficult for a horse, purposely or accidentally, to undo this kind of knot.

A *muck skip* is useful for removing droppings from the stable between muckings out (although a piece of sacking would do) and a *wheelbarrow* helps at mucking-out time, although your yard might provide this. A barrow is not essential; I know of more than one yard where giant muck sheets (circular with a drawstring round the outside) are spread outside the box; muck and badly soiled bedding are dumped in the middle, then the drawstring is pulled close to form a kind of sack, which is then heaved over a burly shoulder whose owner then staggers off to the midden – harder work than a barrow, but cheap.

A *shovel* and *four-tined fork* will be needed for mucking out, and a *rake* will be useful if you are using shavings, sawdust or shredded paper bedding. Finally, you will need a *stable broom* to sweep the yard and the stable itself. The type with real bristles (as opposed to nylon) are best, as they do not clog up with bedding so much. All these might be provided by your yard.

When tying up a haynet, pass the rope through one of the meshes to hoist the net up, tie a half bow, then pass the loose end through the bow, like this, and pull it. This will fasten the net safely and the horse is unlikely to undo it, but it is easy for humans to undo

Grooming kit

Even if your horse is at livery, you will need your own grooming kit. Each horse should have his own to help reduce the spread of any infection such as ringworm, which can occur even in the best yards.

You will need a *dandy brush* with long, stiff bristles to remove dried on stable stains and mud; a *body brush* with short, softer bristles for removing coat grease; a *water brush*, which is not essential but is useful for damping and laying the mane and tail hairs, and which looks like a smaller dandy brush with finer, softer bristles; a *metal curry comb* for cleaning the body brush, not the horse; and maybe a *rubber or plastic curry comb*, which is useful for getting caked mud off the horse. An essential item which you cannot do without is your *hoofpick*. This should be used at every grooming and before and after exercise, also whenever the horse comes in from the field. Use it (as described in Chapter 8) for removing muck, mud and debris such as stones from the underneath of the hooves. You should also have in your kit *two sponges*, a front-end sponge for cleaning eyes, nostrils and lips, and a back-end sponge for sheath (in a gelding), teats (in a mare) and dock. They should be of different colours for easy differentiation, and always kept separate for reasons of hygiene. A final, non-essential item of equipment is a *stable rubber*, which is like a teacloth and is used for giving the coat a final polish and for covering the kit in its bucket or carrying tray (household tidies make good ones) when not in use.

I have not mentioned *hoof oil* and *brush* in the items above because they are not essential, and most hoof oils only succeed in sitting on top of the horn and making everything greasy, not to mention picking up bits. They do not, as is popularly supposed, penetrate the horn and keep it in good condition, but some people like to use them for appearance's sake anyway, an effect which usually lasts only a few minutes, however, depending on the ground surface.

Care

Looking after your tack, harness and clothing is time-consuming but essential to keep it in good, safe condition. It is also very satisfying to see it all hanging gleaming on the tack room wall.

Leatherwork should, strictly speaking, be washed and saddle

soaped after each use, but many people simply don't have the time to do this. To wash your bridle and harness (i.e. anything which is not padded) you can, if you are very pushed for time, simply swish it around in a container – say a plastic dustbin or disused trough – of clean water, as I have seen done by the army and police. This very quickly gets rid of all mud, which could, anyway, scratch the leather if it were rubbed off. If you are not so rushed, wash it thoroughly with a sponge. If it is greasy through being used a few times without cleaning, you will have to sponge off the grease in any case.

Your saddle and any padded items of harness should be washed with a sponge and lukewarm water, which removes grease better than cold, but does not crack the leather, as hot water would. Then either leave them to dry or rub them with a chamois leather.

While the leather is still damp, wipe a separate sponge (just damp, to avoid lathering) on some glycerine saddle soap and then rub the soap thoroughly into the leather, particularly on the 'rough' or inside. (The inside will not be noticeably rough on good-quality leather, in fact.) On the bridle pay special attention to the ends of the cheekpieces inside, which support the bit, and likewise the ends of the reins. It is simpler to remove the bit for this, but there is no real need to dismantle the whole bridle, provided you move the buckles a hole to clean and soap properly those parts that take pressure from the buckles. Properly soaped leather should not feel tacky when finished, and should have a deep sheen.

Driving harness – at least showing harness and especially the collar – is usually boot polished on the outside for extra shine, and soaped on the inside. Metal parts of tack and harness can be cleaned with metal polish (be sure to remove any which gets on the leather), but for obvious reasons do not use it to clean bit mouthpieces. If rings or cheekpieces are polished, they should be thoroughly rinsed afterwards.

You should change over your stirrup leathers each time you clean your saddle. If you constantly have the same one on the left (the side you normally mount from) it will gradually stretch longer than the other and you will find it difficult to get the holes to match up with their opposite number, and therefore to get your stirrups absolutely level.

Fabric items such as numnahs, rugs, blankets and bandages can be washed in a washing machine (either your own or the launderette's – if they will accept your patronage!) with a mild

97

detergent, and given umpteen rinses. Fabric softener in the last rinse helps keep the fabric in good condition and eliminates the rustle and static electricity from synthetic fabrics which can frighten some horses.

Even traditional jute rugs can be washed this way (or soaked and scrubbed by hand in washing soda), provided you oil the leather parts very thoroughly afterwards with a good leather dressing such as Hydrolan. Many people use neatsfoot oil, but I find proprietary dressings better and more pleasant to use. This must also be done after dry cleaning wool day rugs.

If you habitually use glycerine saddle soap on regularly used equipment, you will have no need to oil or dress it unless it is being put away for some months.

Security

Tack and harness thefts are a major problem in some areas. Good equipment is valuable and thieves know this. FarmKey Ltd (see Appendix A) run a tack security scheme in which your tack is marked with a personalized number and a record held in their register; if you lose your tack, or are offered marked tack for sale, details of the rightful owner can be checked with them and the tack returned. Some saddlers also run their own security schemes.

Tack and other equipment should be kept in a secure room or building and under lock and key when not being supervised. You can obtain good, free advice on stableyard and tack security from the Crime Prevention Department of your local police force.

First Aid Kit

The final item of equipment you cannot do without is a first aid kit. A livery yard will undoubtedly have its own, but in practice you cannot beat having your own stock of remedies and equipment and keeping it well stocked with fresh medicines (in other words, products which have not gone beyond the date past which it would be ineffective or unsafe to use them) and the best-quality, most up-to-date products. Your vet is obviously the best person to give you information, and indeed many of the things you need can only be obtained through a vet.

98

Your kit must always be kept clean and hygienic if you don't want to add infection to injury! You will therefore need an easily cleaned and disinfected container such as a plastic carrying chest or a laminate-lined cupboard; also, don't leave tops off containers or let things become contaminated with dirt, bits of bedding or clogged products.

Your vet will probably recommend a range something like this in your kit:

A stubby, veterinary thermometer (not the fine, medical kind)
Bland antiseptic such as Savlon for bathing wounds
Spray or puff-on antibiotic
Non-stick gauze to protect wounds under dressings
Stable and surgical (crepe not gauze) bandages
Colic drench (if your vet advises this – many don't)
Cotton wool or cotton gauze swabs
Gamgee tissue
Poultice dressing (as advised)
Round-ended scissors

It would be advantageous to have self-adhesive bandages, even if only used in strips to keep the crepe ones on, and also, when finances permit, a set of Pressage 'hose'. These are zip-on Lycra contour bandages made to fit awkward areas such as hock and knee.

Do not bother with ointments unless your vet advises them – being cloying, they are hard to remove and can interfere with any care the vet wants to give after your first aid. In some cases, they can prevent wounds knitting together and healing. Also not needed (despite what some of the old school may tell you) are liniments. These were used for massaging into hot or swollen strains and sprains and miraculous claims were made for them: in practice, all they did was facilitate the hand massage needed to apply them and reduce the drag on the skin and hair which occurs without such lubrication. In fact, it is the gentle hand massage which disperses the swelling, not the liniment itself, and most vets these days will tell you that liniments are a waste of money.

Also thoroughly out of favour in the most up-to-date yards are such things as blistering products and 'good (or rather bad!) old red charges'. Recent scientific research has confirmed what many thinking horsepeople had believed for a long time – that blistering and its partner in crime, firing, do not in any way help to heal damaged tendons and liniments. In fact they cause the horse

99

excessive pain, stress and suffering, create further severe injury by burning the skin and underlying tissues, and invite infection and other problems into an already fraught situation. More on this topic can be found in Chapter 8.

8. Care and Management

Dealing with the New Arrival

The big day has arrived! You have chosen your horse, he has passed the vet's inspection, transport and insurance have been arranged, and he is due to arrive at his new home. Whatever else you had arranged for that day, whether it was work, a family outing or some other plan, I hope you will cancel it and make sure you are on the spot when the horse arrives. You need to see that everything is ready for him in his stable or field, and to make sure that you are the first person he sees when that ramp is lowered and he gets the first view of his new world; it is essential that he learns as early as possible that you are his other half – not the staff or whoever else will be looking after him when you are not there, but you.

If you are keeping him elsewhere than at your own home – probably at livery, as I have recommended – you may think it is going to be impossible for the horse to know who you are, but this is not so. Your very attitude to him will be sensed by his acute animal brain and, despite the fact that he sees more of other people than he does of you, he will get to know that you are someone special and will react accordingly. This may be because you handle him in a certain way, or because he does his most interesting things with you on board, but it will be largely a case of extra-sensory perception between you. You, in turn, will become so attuned to him that after a while you will know almost instinctively how he is feeling, what he is going to do next, what he wants to do or what he expects of you.

This idea is not far-fetched. It happens regularly with certain

101

combinations of horse and owner – but it happens just as readily with horse and groom, horse and competition rider or whatever, which is why you must establish bonds early and maintain them afterwards.

When he arrives try to have on the same clothes you wore at your first meeting – you never know, a bell could ring and he just might remember you. Go up the ramp straight to his head and offer him a titbit (having previously found out from his former owner what he likes). Stroke his neck and let him sniff you, talk to him and, being in no rush at all despite your excitement, lead him out. He might pause first to have a look round, so wait with him.

A lot of horses like being fussed, so a welcoming party of interested people would be nice, especially if they have interesting things like apples, Polo mints or other goodies. Incidentally, in my experience it is not a good idea to give a horse sticky things like caramels. I once saw a horse, with its teeth stuck together on a particularly tough caramel, throwing itself around its box in a panic and ending up with several nasty bruises.

Let the horse stand around and have a good look about him. He would probably like to stretch his legs after his journey, so lead him round the yard and then take him to his box. It should be bedded down with completely new bedding and have been thoroughly scrubbed out beforehand so that all traces of previous occupants, as far as possible, have been removed and the horse can mark it as his own, with his own smells, as his very own territory. This is, I feel, rarely done but it is psychologically very important to the newcomer.

Clean, fresh water and hay should be waiting. You should have asked his previous owner for full details of his diet – not only amounts but also times of feeds – and should try to adhere as much as possible to his former routine, changing gradually to the routine of his new yard. Do your best to buy from his other yard a few bales of the hay he has been having and gradually start mixing in with it the sort he will be having in future, so that the microbes in his digestive tract can adjust themselves accordingly and not give him indigestion. This also applies to his concentrate feeds. If he has been eating a certain brand of, say, horse cubes, have the same brand waiting for him, and make any changes very gradually over a period of weeks.

The proprietor of your yard will, if he or she is conscientious and knowledgeable, realize the importance of these gradual changes and will cooperate with you in implementing them. If any reluctance is shown, stress that it is for the horse's good and

102

that he will adjust in a very few weeks. It is not only the physical change of food that can upset him but the psychological change of new people, a new environment and new horses and other animals – all will combine to make him feel lost and strange for a while. First impressions are most important, so do everything you can to make them favourable to him, otherwise he may take a very long time indeed to settle in.

If you can arrange, say, a week of your annual holiday entitlement for this time, you can spend a full week seeing and caring for him every day and he will learn in no uncertain terms that you are his owner; then, even when things get back to normal and other people take over, he will still relate more to you than anyone else. And during this first week you will have more time than the staff to see to his needs and give him the affection he may well need, depending on his temperament.

Once into your normal future routine, whenever you go to the yard make sure you go straight to him and don't stand chatting while he waits for your greeting. Opinions vary as to the advantages or otherwise of feeding titbits. Some people say they cause peevishness and that horses who are used to them only want you for what they can get! Others ask what's wrong with little gifts that you know will be appreciated and believe that, if given in a balanced way and only at certain times, such as on meeting, after work and the like, they cause the horse to associate you with nice things. I tend to agree with the latter view and have never had any problem with horses used to titbits.

One of the Herd

Horses, like humans and other creatures, have a very clearly defined social order and hierarchy, and you can read a great deal about this in books on equine psychology and behaviour (see Appendix B). They make friends and enemies, have superiors and inferiors, and your horse will find his own niche in his new society in time. This will be made easier for him if you introduce him to the other horses in the correct manner. Your yard may well have strict rules about keeping newcomers in isolation for a short time, normally two to three weeks, to give any incubating diseases time to show. This will, I am afraid, probably cause the horse some initial unhappiness, but it is for a good cause and will at least give you and his attendants (his closest contacts) the chance to get to know him and vice versa. In any case, he

103

should be stabled where he can at least see other horses and ponies.

If isolation is not practiced, or when it is over, his introduction to the existing herd must be carried out sensibly. Even horses stabled so they cannot touch each other can have a devastating effect on one another if they are enemies. The inferior one will be unhappy and maybe go off his feed, and will not settle and thrive as he should.

Try to arrange to have your horse stabled next to the one in the yard most likely to accept him – discuss this with the yard proprietor. Once your horse has been allocated a box, try to insist that he keeps it, because moving a horse from box to box, as is done in some yards, really does upset him psychologically unless, of course, a particular box is not to his liking for some reason.

Going for a hack together with his new friend is also an excellent way to introduce two horses under a controlled situation; then turn these two only out together, so that they can form a normal social relationship. Your new horse should be led all round the field fencing and shown the water source in daylight, so he knows where everything is. After his first turn-out period, the other horses should be gradually introduced onto the scene, the most acceptable and sociable ones first. There will be some initial squealing, bottom raising and minor skirmishing until they get to know each other, but you cannot do anything about this. He will just have to stand on his own four feet and learn to fit in.

The most dominant horses in the yard should be introduced last. Your horse will know from the attitude of the others that these particular characters are not to be argued with and will, hopefully, have the sense to conform. It is quite possible, however, that your horse may become one of the more senior animals in the hierarchy himself. Whatever the case, social orders usually sort themselves out and, apart from removing the active troublemakers who cause fights, injuries and virtual nervous breakdowns in timid individuals, there is nothing we humans can do about it. It is obviously stupid to turn loose together animals who have taken an active dislike to each other; where this happens, grazing may have to take place on a rota, or else the animals must be turned out in different paddocks and where they cannot get at each other even over the fence.

Where only two horses are kept together, they can sometimes form such a strong friendship that they become impossible when apart. Here, firm (not vicious) horsemanship is needed to make them both realize that they must learn to work alone, and expert help should be called in when such a situation seems to be developing.

I may seem to have gone into this matter of introductions and social hierarchies in some length, but it is an important topic which is often not given the attention it deserves. Equine psychology and behaviour is a fascinating topic which should be studied closely by everyone who has contact with horses, ponies and donkeys. The Equine Behaviour Study Circle (see Appendix A) is a useful organization for those interested in the subject, and an excellent book on it is recommended in Appendix B.

Feeding

This is probably the most important single topic you will have to master in the care of your horse. Several books have been written solely on this subject, and all good books on management go into it in some detail. Here are the basic elements to enable you to feed your horse adequately without starving or overfeeding him, giving him colic (indigestion or something more serious) or disorders which stem from faulty feeding, such as laminitis, or 'tying-up' (often called azoturia), which are both covered in the veterinary section of this chapter.

Digestive system

The horse evolved as a nomadic animal spending most of his time walking slowly about, grazing for about eighteen hours out of twenty-four. When the pasture in one place was grazed down or becoming littered with horse droppings, the herd moved onto fresh pastures and began again. The horse's natural food, grass and other vegetation, is fibrous and moist and the horse needs to take in substantial quantities to obtain the nourishment he needs. His teeth are extremely powerful, with 'croppers' (incisors) at the front for cutting or tearing off the grass and 'grinders' (molars) at the back for mashing it up to allow entry to saliva, which performs certain chemical changes in the food before it enters the stomach.

In the stomach, more powerful digestive juices chemically break down the grass and other feedstuffs. The horse's stomach is small for the animal's size: because of the horse's eating pattern, the stomach has become geared to receiving small quantities of food frequently, unlike the stomach of a meat-eater which has to be large enough to cope with one large feast every few days (or every day if it is lucky). The stomach works best when two-thirds full (including the digestive juices), which allows the muscles in its wall to work, churning the contents about to aid digestion.

The food is passed on from the stomach into the intestines where different juices work on the food in different sections of what is, in effect, a long tube. The muscles of the intestinal walls squeeze the food along in a wave-like movement called peristalsis until all available nutriment has been extracted and transported by the bloodstream and lymphatic system to various parts of the body, either for further processing (such as in the liver), for immediate use (such as in muscles) or for storage (such as in the various fat deposits around the body). The waste material left is pushed out of the far end of the tube as the horse's droppings (of which the horse will pass about eight piles in twenty-four hours depending on the type of diet) and other waste products are excreted by the kidneys in the urine.

The type and pattern of feeding described above must be adhered to as closely as possible in the stabled or partly stabled horse if you want to ensure his contentment and wellbeing. The artificially high levels of work demanded of high-performance horses such as eventers, racehorses and endurance horses are not unreasonable provided these animals are fed accordingly. If people tried to work such horses off grass alone, they would find that the horse needed to eat impossibly large amounts of it to get the required level of nutrients, thus (even if it were possible) overloading the digestive system with vast amounts of bulk which the poor horse would have to haul around during his work.

To overcome this, working horses are fed more concentrated, drier food such as hay and grain (oats, barley and maize) so that the animals receive the right amount of nourishment but in less volume. However, the horse cannot change his physical characteristics just because we change his food, and his intestines still need bulk, so adequate bulky roughage must also be included in his diet.

This fibrous roughage, which is provided mainly in hay, is needed to break up the more concentrated food (grain etc.) physically so that the digestive juices can get in and process the food chemically, making it suitable for absorption into the blood and lymph. If roughage were not fed, the concentrates would impact into a stiff, gooey mass which could not be digested and

106

which would eventually ferment; the gases then produced would cause a ruptured intestine – a fatal occurrence – or reabsorption of toxic substances.

To cater for both the horse's digestive needs and our own requirement for him to obtain enough nourishment to do our work, therefore, we have to balance carefully the amounts of roughage and concentrates we feed. For a horse doing moderately active work, such as two hours' hacking comprising mostly walking with trotting and some fast work, per day we should aim to divide his diet into about two-thirds roughage and one-third concentrates. As will be described below, no food consists entirely of roughage or entirely of concentrates – good hay, for example, is a complete feed for horses in slow work or resting. However as a practical guide, if you give your horse two-thirds of his total daily feed-weight requirements as hay (part of which might be chop – see p. 112) and one-third as concentrates such as grains, cubes (nuts) or coarse mix, the health of his digestive system should be catered for and an adequate level of nourishment provided for work as well.

Uses of food
The horse's body has to be maintained very close to its optimum working temperature and has to have enough resources to maintain itself, otherwise the animal will die, so the first two uses below take priority over the others:

1. Maintenance of body temperature at around 38°C (100·4°F).

2. Production of body tissue such as muscle, skin, horn, hair, bone etc.

3. Putting on condition and weight, or storing surplus feed as fat, to be called on as needed when requirements exceed supply, for instance when the horse is being fed insufficiently to keep out the cold or provide for the work being demanded of him.

4. To provide energy for life processes (everything from heart-beat to hormone production) and movement, strength and stamina.

In terms of food usage, 'work' can mean anything from the horse's shaking his head to get rid of flies or ambling over to the water trough to chasing a rival off the choicest piece of grass, through taking you for a relaxing hack or drive, to jumping the Coffin at Badminton or getting his nose first past the winning post at Epsom. His body works just like a car engine – the more work it does, the faster it goes and the longer it continues, the more fuel (feed) it needs. A car, of course, will stop without fuel; a horse will keep going but something else will suffer – usually requirement no. 3 above will suffer and the horse will lose an undue amount of condition.

If you continue to work a horse hard on insufficient food, or expose him to harsh winter weather without enough nourishment to enable him to keep up his body temperature (incidentally, in some conditions it can be impossible for him to maintain his temperature without the added facility of a shelter shed), the reserves of fat become depleted and the body starts using up its own tissue and wasting away. Ultimately, body temperature drops and the horse dies.

Feeding too much will make the horse dangerously obese, cause circulatory problems and subject him to the same unnecessary strains as a fat human.

Feed requirements

Feed according to bodyweight, not height. On average horses and ponies will eat 2 lb per 100 lb bodyweight (2 kg/100 kg). Ponies with a tendency to fat generally require less feed per 100 lb bodyweight than horses.

To estimate your horse or pony's bodyweight, take the girth measurement at a quiet time, right around the barrel. The tape should lie in the girth groove and just behind the withers. Read off the measurement when the animal finishes breathing out.

The tables opposite are offered as guidelines, it is best to check cob-types against the tables on a public weighbridge to find which table applies to them. The tables illustrate that just ½ inch (1.23 cm) change in girth can mean 14–15 lb (5–6 kg) change in bodyweight, which may not be visible to the naked eye.

Once your horse or pony is fit, you should feed to maintain bodyweight throughout the season.

For example, a pony with girth measurement 55 inches with an approx bodyweight of 502 lb will require 10 lb of feed per day. If this pony is a typical Native Pony doing light work, the feed will therefore be 25% concentrate 75% forage. So the pony will receive approx 7 lb hay and 3 lb of concentrates.

Body condition

It is important that you learn to judge when a horse is in good condition, which varies for the type of work he is doing, and when he is too thin or too fat, which must be related to his body type. A stockily built cob, for instance, may look fat compared to an Arab of the same height, yet they could both be in good

108

Table 1. Ponies

Girth in inches	40	42.5	45	47.5	50	52.5	55	57.5
Girth in cm	101	108	114	120	127	133	140	146
Bodyweight in lb	100	172	235	296	368	430	502	562
Bodyweight in kg	45	77	104	132	164	192	234	252

Table 2. Horses

Girth in inches	55	57.5	60	62.5	65	67.5
Girth in cm	140	146	152	159	165	171
Bodyweight in lb	538	613	688	776	851	926
Bodyweight in kg	240	274	307	346	380	414

Girth in inches	70	72.5	75	77.5	80	82.5
Girth in cm	178	184	190	199	203	206
Bodyweight in lb	1014	1090	1165	1278	1328	1369
Bodyweight in kg	453	486	520	570	593	611

(Tables based on work of Glushanok, Rochlitz & Skay, 1981)

condition for their types. Endurance horses may look positively scrawny compared to show hacks, but their condition is right for their work. If you watch a variety of equestrian events, from racing to showing, as often as possible, and assess the condition of the best animals taking part, you will gradually develop an eye for condition.

In winter, when horses and particularly ponies grow long, thick coats, dig your fingers through the coat to the ribs, hips and spine beneath. The hair disguises poor condition, so make sure you can feel plenty of flesh over the bones (but can still feel where the bones are)!

Constituents of feed
Water is more vital to life than any solid feed; without water a horse will die within a very few days. His body is about 70 per cent water: all the body tissues are bathed in fluid; the cells (hollow 'bricks') making up the body are filled with fluid; and the blood is largely liquid, as are the digestive juices and the lymph,

109

the synovia (joint oil) lubricating your horse's joints and a mare's milk to feed her foal. Water is also a constituent of sweat, which is important in helping to regulate body temperature by evaporation and in excreting toxic waste products via the skin, and urine. In short, next to air, your horse needs water more than anything else on earth.

All feeds contain some water to a greater or lesser degree, but nothing like enough for a horse's full requirements. Without an adequate supply (which can vary from six to fifteen gallons a day depending on whether he is a Shetland or a Shire, the work he is doing and the surrounding temperature), his body will draw on its own fluid content. He will thus become dehydrated, seriously ill and even die if his condition is not corrected.

Carbohydrates are the starches and sugars vital for producing energy and heat; surplus carbohydrate is stored as fat. It is found mainly in cereal grains such as barley, maize (which is nearly all starch), oats, cubes, coarse mixes, bran, hay and hay-age products, coarse grass and feed additives like molasses and honey. Carbohydrates and fats (energy foods) *cannot* be turned into protein.

Proteins are the only foods able to manufacture body tissue, but can also provide some heat and energy for work. Protein as such cannot be stored by the body, so a daily supply is needed. Required in lesser amounts than carbohydrates, protein is found in many of the same feedstuffs as carbohydrates, but foods especially noted for protein content are beans and peas (not commonly fed), linseed, clover and other legume plants, milk powder, young grass and special protein supplements.

Fat is good for producing heat and energy and it is now believed that horses can not only tolerate but actually thrive on higher-fat diets than previously recommended. Vegetable oils and fats are added to many made-up, compound feeds such as nuts and coarse mixes, and boiled linseed is still widely fed in many stables, although the need for it has largely been superseded by the new compounds. Nevertheless, many horses love it mixed in their feed, especially on a cold night. Animal fats should never be fed to horses. Most cereals naturally contain some fat. High-fat diets should also be high in Vitamin E and choline to ensure adequate breakdown.

Fibre, also known as roughage and bulk, is needed for reasons already given. It gives your horse that satisfied, full feeling that we all expect after a meal and is mainly supplied by means of hay and hay-age. Basically, fibre is the hard, woody portion of

110

vegetable matter and there are two types: cellulose, which can be digested to a certain extent and is a form of carbohydrate, and lignin, which is indigestible and will be excreted, but which forms a valuable mechanical service in stimulating the movements of the intestine and physically breaking up concentrate foods.

Vitamins, minerals and trace elements are needed in small quantities but are essential for adequate processing of other foods and for various body functions too complex to go into here. Imbalances of these substances can cause serious problems in horses, and supplements containing them should never be used indiscriminately. Many compound feeds contain correctly balanced amounts of vitamins, minerals and trace elements and an additional supplement should not be needed. However, owners who prefer to feed 'straights' (oats, barley, maize or other grains, backed up by bran) often unknowingly run into trouble in the form of a deficiency of one substance or an excess of another. The result can range from a horse who simply does not perform at his best to one who develops bone disorders – usually from an excess of phosphorus, eg through feeding too much bran.

Most foods used for horses contain varying amounts of several of the constituents discussed, and balancing a diet can be a major headache for an inexperienced owner. In any case, it is not possible unless you have at your disposal (and can understand!) a proper analysis of the foodstuffs, and for this reason I recommend first-time owners to use ready-mixed compound feeds of a reputable make and also not to use any feed supplements without first talking to an equine nutritionist/horse management consultant (see Equine Management Consultancy Service, Appendix A) or a vet.

Types of feeds
Hay is probably the foundation food of most horses, and, as mentioned above, good hay can be enough on its own for horses doing light to moderate work. Apart from its nutritional value, hay is your horse's entertainment, and apart from hay-age (see p. 112) is the nearest a stabled horse can get to feeding as nature intended, steadily and constantly.

It takes more chewing than concentrates and can provide a horse with many hours of contentment and occupation. Horses should not be fed too soon before working (see p. 117, Rules of feeding), but at other times I see no reason why they should not have a constant supply of hay available. They will only eat what

111

they need and will not gorge themselves on it, as some horses do on concentrates, so it is not going to cost any more money.

There are various types of hay, but for most horses good meadow hay, containing a palatable variety of grasses, and no poisonous weeds like ragwort or mare's tails, is the kind to ask for. Other hays which you may come across are seed or racehorse hay, which is specially sown as a crop and is protein-rich; mixture hay, which is a mixture of seed and meadow hay; clover hay, which is high in protein but dusty and bitty, as are the rarer hays lucerne and sainfoin; and ryegrass and timothy hays, both of which consist almost exclusively of the grasses which give them their name.

Hay-age is, as its name implies, a cross between hay, which is basically fairly mature dried cut grass, and silage, which is basically wetter, less mature cut grass which is 'pickled' in its own juices. Hay-age comes under various brand names such as Hygrass and Horsehage, vacuum packed and sealed in tough polythene sacks. It can therefore be stored outside and so releases valuable storage space for other purposes. Care must be taken not to puncture the bags, however, or the product can deteriorate to the point at which it becomes dangerous to feed.

The advantage of hay-age over hay exists mainly for horses prone to wind (respiratory) allergies such as wheezing, chronic coughs and breathlessness. These symptoms are signs of a condition called chronic obstructive pulmonary disease (COPD), otherwise known as broken wind, heaves or emphysema. It is caused by moulds or fungal spores in hay and straw, to which some individuals are susceptible. Even good samples of fodder can contain these spores, which are invisible to the naked eye.

To introduce hay-age to a horse only used to hay, mix in a very small amount with his hay ration, gradually increasing the amount and cutting down the hay, over a period of about three weeks. Once used to it, many horses prefer it to hay.

Chop is hay and/or straw cut up small (about 2 cm long) and mixed in with the concentrate feeds. It is useful for making greedy horses chew their food properly and for adding essential bulk to a meal. Sometimes called 'chaff', it can be bought from merchants along with your other feedstuffs and cut on your own premises, if you have a chaff-cutter, or bought as a brand-name product such as Mollichaff, ready-mixed with molasses for palatability and to keep the dust down.

Cubes or nuts were introduced onto the British market twenty-odd years ago following their success with cattle, and are, indeed, very convenient. If stored in cool, dry conditions they keep for several weeks and a good make will contain balanced quantities of vitamins, minerals and other constituents.

Coarse mixes are a more recent addition to the market but are becoming very popular. They are particularly recommended for novice owners, rather unkindly, I feel, as being idiotproof, which simply means that the owner need only weigh out the appropriate amount (guided by the manufacturer's instructions) according to the size/weight of his or her horse, for the animal to receive the correct amount of a good, balanced diet. (I can think of several so-called experts who could do with this type of feed, never mind novices!) There are several makes available; at the time of writing two good ones are marketed by Dodson and Horrell and Belvoir Horse Feeds.

Oats have for generations been considered the staple concentrate for horses in Britain and most other western countries. Hay, oats and bran have been *de rigueur* for animals of all types, and it has been, and in some quarters still is, felt that those three foods plus a little of whatever you fancy will do your horse good, such as carrots, eggs, stout, treacle, honey and so on, are all that a horse could need or want.

Over the last decade or so, however, a minor revolution has taken place in horse feeding as a result of research, and it is now known that horses eating oats, hay and bran as their staple diet can, according to the quality and analysis of the individual batches of feeds in use, be on some of the most unbalanced diets around. Some conscientious yards, notably professional ones such as racing yards but also high-class amateur yards such as eventers', do have their feeds analysed by a laboratory and formulate a diet, possibly containing supplements, as needed. However many others do not, which results in their horses being fed a haphazardly made-up diet which is very likely to be unbalanced. Their horses may look and perform well, but they would look and perform so much better if advantage were taken of up-to-date knowledge.

Oats are palatable, easy to chew if lightly crushed or rolled to crack the outside, fibrous husk, and contain, in a good sample, fairly well-balanced amounts of carbohydrate, protein and other feed constituents; they will therefore continue in use indefinitely. They can have an intoxicating effect on some horses, and they definitely add a zip to sluggish horses and those in hard work. Some horses, however, become impossibly silly on them and others develop skin problems, and for such individuals barley

113

would be a better grain. They are also deficient in an important protein constituent – lysine.

Barley keeps horses calmer, in practice, but can be very success-ful. It must be fed rolled or bruised as it is hard and unlikely to be chewed properly if fed whole. Ready-cooked, flaked barley is also available. Some people boil or steam the whole grains and use them for sick or tired horses. While many horses do love cooked feeds, the reasons for feeding them can now be covered by the modern feeds on the market, although their popularity with many horses is reason enough for giving them as a treat.

Bran is probably most famous for its use in bran mashes, which are usually recommended to be fed to sick horses or to those off work. They are often given to horses before a rest day when they might be standing in all day – a thoroughly bad practice in my view, and unfair to an active animal such as a horse. The facts are, as mentioned earlier, that bran, when fed in the sort of quantities most owners use, can result in an excess of phosphorus in the diet. This can cause bone disorders, and bran mashes them-selves, far from being the easily digested diet they are said to be, are in fact highly indigestible. It is true that they do have a laxative effect on horses, but this purging effect is achieved because they are hard to digest, rather than the other way round.

If owners wish to use a little bran, damped, to help distribute, say, worming powders among a feed, no harm will be done, but it should not comprise more than a sixth by weight of the whole concentrate feed, and should be balanced with a calcium-rich feed. Most horses would be better off without bran in their diet in significant quantities. If a 'false' feed is desired for the sake of routine on days when the horse is not working, use instead chop plus thinly sliced roots such as carrots, or sugar beet pulp which has been soaked in twice its own volume of water for twenty-four hours before feeding. Alternatively, for longer lay-offs you might find that the firm making your brand of coarse mix or cubes has an 'invalid' feed for sick or resting horses, which will not cause the problems associated with overfeeding. Remember, too, that, with false feed, it is best to have a little of each ingredient from 'normal' feed in 'day-off' feeds to keep digestive bugs going.

Maize is usually fed cooked and flaked and, being nearly all starch, is good for putting weight on thin horses or providing energy. However, it should only form part of the concentrate ration, and not be the main ingredient.

Where to buy
If you are buying branded feeds such as cubes or a coarse mix, you may well be able to get your supplies from saddlers, many of whom, particularly the supermarket type of firm, now sell such products. Normally, however, the best place would probably be a good feed merchant, who can also supply you with your hay and bedding, plus straight feeds such as oats, barley etc. You may have no problems if your livery yard buys in its own supplies, but if you are responsible for purchasing your own feed, ask your adviser to recommend a good merchant, look in the Yellow Pages directory for local firms (probably under 'Animal Feed Merchants'), in the British Equestrian Directory under 'Feed' or 'Hay and Corn Merchants' or contact the British Hay and Straw Merchants' Association (see Appendix A) to ask if they have a member firm near you.

Judging quality
Horses have very delicate digestions, and you cannot risk feeding them any food which is even slightly off. Your best practical guide to judging feed quality is your nose. All feed should smell either of nothing or positively sweet and appetizing. If any food – hay, oats, coarse mix or whatever – smells sour or musty, don't touch it. If feed is delivered to you in this condition, send it back. If it is delivered during your absence, ring up the merchant as soon as possible and say it is to be collected. As most concentrate feeds are delivered in tied or sealed bags, you should really open at least one of them and test the quality before you sign for the batch, but most people don't. Despite this, a reputable merchant will exchange it for you after your complaint, and you can cause trouble, through your consumer rights, if they don't.

Hay should be greenish to golden with closed seed heads and be leafy and bright, not dull, stemmy, brown or yellow, with open seed heads, known as 'gone to seed'; when you cut the twine a bale should spring open rather than dropping lifelessly apart. There should be no suspicion of white or black spots of mould or damp on it (the same goes for straw for bedding) or dust when shaken out; and it should have a sweet aroma.

Storage
Food should generally be stored in a cool, dry, well-ventilated place. Hay kept in open-sided barns, however, if exposed to the rain, can quickly be ruined. Concentrates are best kept in galvanized bins or – a good substitute – plastic dustbins, and

where horses and vermin cannot gain access. Do not store feed of any kind or straw where dust can get at it, such as round the edges of an indoor school or near a dusty outdoor manège or cinder track, or in direct sunlight. Also, protect it from rats etc., especially if you put down rat poison as they may eat poison and die in the feed bin.

Methods of feeding

As described, the horse's digestive system works best when small quantities of food pass through it frequently. It is generally held that for an average-sized horse (whatever that is) rather than a pony, not more than about 4 lb (say 2 kg) should be given in one concentrate feed, as this is enough for the stomach to take in one go. If, therefore, your horse needs more concentrates than this they will have to be given in two feeds, three or four, spread over the day and evening, depending on his ration. It is generally felt best to give the largest feed at night when the horse has time to digest it.

Hay, however, passes through the stomach more quickly than concentrates, being digested mainly further down the intestinal tract, and a more or less constant supply can and should be left with the horse, except before work. Horses should not be fed less than about two hours before work, certainly fast work, as this can cause digestive and respiratory troubles.

Concentrates should be thoroughly mixed and, if bran is used, the feed should be damped slightly as dry bran can cause choking. Do not prepare feeds with dirty or smelly hands as this can put a horse off his feed quite easily.

Weigh feed accurately on a pair of kitchen scales to avoid under- or overfeeding. Hay scales (the spring-balance type) should be used for weighing hay, too. (These can be bought from most angling shops). You can either hang your net on the hook, or put your hay on an opened out sack and hang the four corners on the hook.

Keep mangers and buckets clean and scrubbed and thoroughly rinsed, to avoid a build-up of stale, rotting food.

Water can be given in automatic drinkers provided they are checked regularly, at least twice a day, and cleaned out. Buckets can also be used; if you use two and site them in different corners of the box, downhill of the slope of the floor in case they get knocked over, you will make sure that your horse will have at least one clean bucket available if, as often happens, he does a dropping in the other! Like hay, water should be constantly with the horse. Re-fill, don't 'top-up', as ammonia from the stable makes water 'flat' and unpalatable.

Many owners fit a salt lick and holder in their stables for the horse to get his own supply. In hot weather, however, about one to four dessertspoonfuls of salt can be added to each feed to guarantee adequate intake, depending on work load.

Golden rules of feeding
1. *Feed little and often*, for reasons already given.
2. *Water before feeding*. This applies for horses who do not have water always with them. However, for novice owners it is safer to leave water always with the horse and, indeed, most western horses are kept this way. In this way horses will not overdrink, and the short drink which many will take after a feed will not cause the digestive problems which could result if a long draught were taken after a feed.
3. *Make any changes in feeds, amounts or times gradually* over a period of days or weeks, to give the digestive system a chance to adjust.
4. *Use only good-quality food*. Bad food can cause illness and is also uneconomical as it will have a low nutrient content.
5. *Feed something succulent*, such as carrots, a turnip, soaked sugar beet pulp or whatever else the horse likes, every day, particularly when the horse has no access to grass, to satisfy the natural craving for moist, juicy food.
6. *Feed according to temperament and work, and according to climate and weather*. Overfeeding is as common as and often worse than underfeeding, so learn to judge your horse's requirements accurately.
7. *Do not work fast or hard straight after feeding*. If your horse has been in the field, and therefore eating grass, walk for the first half hour, and do no fast work, such as cantering or jumping, for at least an hour. After a stable feed, give the horse at least an hour to begin to digest it before work.
8. *Keep to a routine* and feed at the same times each day whenever possible. However there are times, such as show days or when the horse is travelling, when this cannot be maintained, and in practice, provided horses are not allowed to get really hungry (by making sure that they usually have hay), they are not unduly upset by being fed at odd times.

How much to give?
This is a vexed question for many owners, but you will soon get to

know your own horse or pony. There is a very rough guide which will at least give you some idea of what to budget for and buy in. Take the height of your animal in hands, double it and take the answer as pounds weight. This will be on the generous side, so knock off a few pounds and you have your answer, which you can then convert into kilograms. For instance, if you have a 15 hands high animal, double 15 is 30 lb, which is 13·6 kg. Reduce this a bit and you will have a fairly safe ration. This is the total daily food weight requirement, so if you do as recommended earlier and split this into two-thirds roughage (hay or hay-age) and one-third concentrates (cubes, coarse mix etc.) you will not go far wrong.

A much more accurate way is to feed according to body weight. But your horse will not fit on the bathroom scales and you may not have a weighbridge nearby. So how do you weigh your horse? You can buy special tapes, just like roll-up tape measures, which you pass round your horse's girth and which are graduated so that you can simply read off his approximate weight and consequent daily food requirement. They are available by post from the Equine Management Consultancy Service (see Appendix A) and are sometimes advertised in equestrian journals. Good saddlers might also sell them.

Food analysis
Having each batch of your feed analysed, particularly if using straight feeds, is the only real way of knowing just what you are feeding your horse. Unfortunately, the analysis will mean next to nothing to most owners, particularly novices, so a little guidance might be welcomed.

You should look for feeds which say on their analysis labels that they contain 10–12 MJ (megajoules) of digestible energy (DE) per kilogram. If the bag does not say anything along these lines, contact the manufacturers and ask for confirmation. For ponies, cobs and animals in light work, 8·5–10 MJ per kg is adequate.

An important point worth remembering in relation to the formula given above, to formulae you may read in books or, indeed, any other advice on gauging quantities of feed, is that animals with plenty of pony or cob blood are usually what are called 'good doers'. This means that they do not require much food to keep them in good condition. In fact, such animals often become dangerously fat on diets quite suitable for other horses, especially when on spring and summer grass.

For light to moderate work (say up to two hours' fairly active hacking per day – walking, trotting, cantering, perhaps a spin at a faster pace, and a little jumping) animals of this type often do very nicely on nothing but good hay. If they are in a yard where other horses are being given 'short' feeds (concentrates) they can be given a false feed as described earlier, so that they don't feel left out. If they are quite fat enough but sluggish, 1–2 lb ($\frac{1}{2}$–1 kg) of oats could be given and other food cut down a little. Their grazing should be of poor quality. It is imperative to avoid overweight, or laminitis (see the veterinary section of this chapter) could certainly result.

Bedding

We provide bedding to stabled horses to help keep them clean and warm, to encourage them to lie down and rest, and to provide them with standing which is not unnaturally hard but which feels more like earth. Animals turned out on an area offering a choice of turf or concrete (say in the gateway or round the shelter) do not choose to lie on the concrete!

The object of good bed management is to provide a thick, dry, clean bed, although you may find this hard to believe when you look at the thin, damp or dirty mess on which some horses, even in supposedly reputable yards, have to stand and lie.

One of the main secrets of good bedding management is to remove droppings as soon as possible. Of course, during the night this is hardly possible, but during the day, in a properly staffed yard, the following old maxim should be adhered to:

One pile of droppings – permissible

Two piles of droppings – reprimand the groom

Three piles of droppings – dismiss him or her

When keeping your horse at livery you cannot dismiss the staff, but if you regularly find your horse or pony on an inadequate bed you surely have cause for a politely but firmly expressed complaint. (I realize all too well that complaints about livery service can result in your being given notice to quit, and that in many areas livery stables have waiting lists as long as their arms, but the fact remains that you should learn what are and what are not acceptable standards in all areas of management, so that you can take whatever action is open to you to rectify matters.)

Another way to keep your horse's bed in good order is to lay it on a well-drained base, such as the mesh flooring mentioned in

119

Chapter 3 or loose-weave asphalt flooring. If this is not possible, your bedding will inevitably become wet as your horse stales on it and, as today's bedding materials are all of the type known as 'absorbent bedding' which, as their name suggests, absorb moisture, little or none of it will drain to the outside, no matter how well grooved or sloped your floor is. The only type of bedding in the other category ('drainage bedding') was old-fashioned straw, with its round, hard stems off which urine would run. Today's combined straw, however, is crushed up, sometimes to little more than a pulp, and its split stems absorb urine almost as readily as other beddings.

Materials
Readily available in Britain are straw, wood shavings, sawdust, peat and shredded or diced paper.

If you can get good *straw*, your bed will look bright, fluffy and inviting. Too often, however, straw is mouldy and damp and quite unsuitable. Some greedy animals and also those not receiving enough good hay will readily eat straw, ingest the mould and give themselves various disorders, particulary respiratory ones – and an athletic animal such as a horse needs good lungs as much as he needs good feet and legs. Even good straw, as mentioned earlier, contains a few mould spores – enough to cause problems in allergy-prone animals.

Wood shavings are popular, but some people find them difficult to manage, and shavings beds are often damp if you investigate underneath the top layer. They are, however, better for 'windy' horses than straw, particularly the dust-extracted type.

Sawdust is not so common but can make a good bed. Pine sawdust, if you can get it, gives your stable a lovely perfume!

Peat is one material with which I have never had any success. There are two types of peat, sedge peat and sphagnum moss peat. The latter, in particular, is said to absorb up to nine times its own weight in moisture. I have always found peat beds very difficult to keep dry; therefore, they are cold, and even prone to freezing in winter. In summer, because they hold urine, they smell and give off dangerous ammonia fumes. Even for well-ventilated, well-drained stables I do not recommend peat.

Shredded or diced paper is particularly good for horses with allergy problems, as it does not contain moulds or the residues of chemical sprays which are sometimes found on wood shavings or sawdust, having been absorbed by the trees from which these products come. At the time of writing, however, recent research stresses that paper bedding is not recommended for deep litter systems (see overleaf) because it is very absorbent and, like peat, can hold urine. However, paper dries out very quickly, and if managed on a semi-deep litter system, as recommended by most of its suppliers, and tossed and turned to dry daily, it does make good bedding.

This problem of chemical residues and mould spores is always with us today. Some horses are more prone to disorders from them than others, and you may well need to try a variety of bedding materials until you find the right one for your horse.

Disposal of manure

There are three main methods of muck disposal. One is to give it away to get rid of it quickly in urban areas, the second is to let it rot down very thoroughly indeed and then use it on your paddocks, and the third and most common one is to sell it to a nursery, most commonly a mushroom grower. If you put a sign outside your front gate advertising odd bags for sale you could be faced with either an endless stream of keen gardeners down your path at inconvenient times or a steadily increasing muck heap which is fast becoming a threat to the health of the local population!

Some nurseries are fussy and will not take paper. However, there was a time when they would not take shavings, but they had to relent as more and more horse owners turned to it in the absence of good straw. If you have to make your own disposal arrangements, ring several nurseries to discover what they will take. If all else fails and you cannot even give it away, you may have to burn it.

Bedding systems

There are three main systems of bedding:
1. Full mucking out and bedding down.
2. Semi-deep litter.
3. Deep litter.

In the first system, the droppings and wettest bedding are removed with a shovel and four-tine fork (the best sort for this job); the part-clean and clean straw (straw being the most suitable material for this system) are put in two piles; the floor is thoroughly swept – and washed and disinfected too, if time – and the part-clean straw is laid back on the floor. The clean stuff is laid on top and fresh straw is brought in and put on top of that, plus

121

being banked up around the sides of the box to a height of about 2 feet to give extra protection and warmth.

In the second system, suitable for all other materials, the droppings are removed plus the badly soiled bedding. Semi-clean material is raked in (garden rakes are good for this) from the banks round the sides, and fresh bedding is put on top. With paper, the bed is tossed to one side to air while the horse is out. This is a good practice to follow with any material, actually.

In the third system, droppings only are removed and the temptation resisted to take out wet bedding, too. This may sound grossly unhygienic, but in practice deep litter makes a springy, warm bed provided your stable is very well ventilated and not prone to gathering moisture. Fresh bedding is laid, a little every day, and as the bed becomes established you will be less and less conscious that there is a lower layer. When deep litter beds are taken out every few months (that's right!) the material underneath is often found to be quite dry and rotted, and not objectionable at all. If the stable floor has been laid on damp foundations, however, it will be a squelchy, stinking mess of which you will have become highly conscious long ago!

Amount to use

It is sometimes difficult for the inexperienced to gauge the right amount of bedding to provide adequate buffering and warmth without being unduly extravagant. With straw it is easy – just thrust the fork down through the bed; if the tines hit the floor the bed is too thin. With other materials, which scatter more easily than straw, it is not so easy. Again, the fork test can be used; the bedding should cover the tines, but as other materials do not have the cushioning effect of straw, you will still be able to reach the floor.

This is one of the reasons why other bedding materials are often used on semi-deep litter so that there is an established, relatively stable layer underneath, to resist scattering by the horse's hooves.

As a final test, when you walk into a stable you should feel that you are walking on a firm cushion, not on bedding with a hard floor underneath.

Grooming

The amount of grooming your horse should receive depends on how he is kept and the work he is doing. In practice, a regularly
122

worked horse is much easier to keep clean than an idle, unfit one. This is because exercise tones up the whole body, including the skin, which is therefore fairly effective at keeping itself clean and in good working order. A comparatively idle skin holds grease and dirt, which then needs considerable human elbow grease to remove it. Grass-kept horses, whether working or not, should not be heavily body brushed as this removes too much protective grease from their coats. For the same reason it is also not a good plan to shampoo them.

Having said that, a stabled horse on an artificial diet of concentrates must be groomed to help keep his skin in good order, for a healthy skin is instrumental in helping to regulate body temperature through sweat and in helping to excrete metabolic waste products.

Quartering is a quick brush-over with the dandy brush to remove stable stains and bedding before exercise. The feet are also picked out.

Grooming is normally done after exercise when the horse is dry but still warm. Many people like to hose off mud as this makes subsequent grooming easier. Old (and some not so old) books say you should let mud dry on and then brush it off – otherwise your horse will get cracked (chapped) legs and heels. I know several veterinary surgeons who think this a slovenly practice and who advise that mud, with its present-day chemical content, should always be rinsed off, the belly, legs and heels, dried thoroughly with old towels, maybe a hand hair-dryer and stable bandages to avoid chapping, and the horse then groomed.

Begin body brushing at the head and work back and down all over your horse, using a routine area by area so that nowhere is forgotten. The parts usually missed and which harbour dirt are under the forelock and mane, under the breast and belly, between the legs, behind the pasterns and under the tail.

Have your body brush in one hand and your metal curry comb in the other, and have your brush-arm elbow slightly bent but stiff. Then brush by leaning your weight on your arm, rather than pushing which is very tiring. Six long, firm strokes in one place should be enough. After two or three strokes, draw the bristles firmly over the curry comb to extract dirt, and every now and then tap the comb on its side near the door or outside to dislodge the grease and dandruff.

Be gentle around the head and bony and sensitive areas, or your horse may become difficult to groom. Never scrub these areas with the dandy brush.

Brush out the forelock, mane and tail, one lock at a time and right from the roots, using the body brush which is the best one for removing grease. Damp-sponge the front and back ends with their respective sponges (eyes, nostrils and lips, then sheath or teats and dock) and dry with a towel, if necessary.

Pick out the hooves with the hoofpick, working from heel to toe, and being sure to remove gently but firmly all muck, mud and debris from the underside of the feet. To pick up a hind foot, stand facing the tail and run your hand from the quarter (rump) down the back of the leg to the fetlock, put your hand round the front of the pastern, say 'Up' firmly and pull upwards, when a well-mannered horse will lift his foot for you. To pick up a front foot, run your hand from the shoulder down the back of the leg and do likewise.

If your horse is very dirty and you need to *shampoo* him, use warm (neither hot nor cold) water, a proper animal shampoo or mild washing up liquid, and avoid his head. Soap him all over with a large sponge, rinse very thoroughly indeed and rub him dry with straw or old towels. If the weather is warm, lead him round to dry. If it is chilly, put straw or a mesh anti-sweat rug under an old rug or tied-on sacking, apply bandages on his legs, and make certain his legs and heels are properly dry. Never shampoo in cold weather.

Clipping
If you have only one horse it is scarcely worthwhile your buying a clipping machine, as you can pay a professional to clip your horse. It is no job for a novice, anyway. As mentioned earlier, some coat will have to be removed if your horse is working in winter, but for most 'hobby' horses an Irish or trace clip, or at most a blanket clip, is quite adequate. Your horse must be clean and dry before starting or the clippers will blunt, overheat and pull the hair, making the horse fractious and difficult.

A clipped animal will need clothing to compensate for the loss of coat, so make sure you have a supply of rugs and blankets, as appropriate. To check if a horse is cold, feel the base of his ears and his loins. If they feel chilly, then he is, too. If he is very warm and maybe even sweating, he is too hot, so remove some of his clothing.

This is a hunter clip (with the saddle patch and legs left on). It is suitable for hard-working horses with thick coats, who would sweat excessively if too much hair were left on

Feet and Shoes

If you want your horse to work well for you, you must see that he is comfortable in his feet. Correctly balanced feet, which were discussed in Chapter 6, is what a good farrier will aim at when attending to your horse. Not all horses need shoes if they work mainly on smooth or soft surfaces, but expert trimming is still needed to retain this all-important balance and prevent the feet becoming overgrown and uneven.

Most animals do have shoes, however, and, although it is not easy in some areas, you should do your best to obtain the services of the best farrier available. This can be tricky if you keep your horse at a school or livery yard who has a particular farrier whose work is not of the best (and such people do exist, despite qualifications, although the general standard is improving). As an independent owner, however, you should be free to choose

125

An Irish clip, very useful for fine-coated horses and those in light work, or spending long days at grass in winter (wearing a New Zealand rug) while their owners are at work. This clip still allows such horses to work hard enough to be made fit for moderately hard work such as active hacking and light hunting, and could be made more use of than it is

your farrier and vet. Vets think of their clients as individuals and it is quite common for communal yards to be visited by different vets, but the situation seems to be different with farriers, unfortunately. You may have great difficulty in persuading a farrier to see to your horse or pony if he is kept at a yard served by a different one. Make it clear from the beginning with the proprietor and the farrier that you will have the farrier you want, provided you can get him. Particularly if the farrier is aware that you are a new client at that yard and have never used the existing man, you should have no trouble.

If you use a farrier who stays at his forge and does not travel, as do most farriers, there will be no problem except that of transporting your horse to the forge if it is not within hacking distance.

If your adviser or yard proprietor cannot fix you up with a well-recommended farrier, contact the Farriers' Registration Council (see Appendix A) and ask for details of farriers practising within a reasonable distance of your horse's home. Again, personal recommendation from other horse owners is often a good guide. It is worth using a distant farrier if your local man's work is inadequate.

Shoeing process
Your farrier should first study your horse's feet and legs and his action to assess his way of going and consequent requirements. Tell him what work you are doing and ask for advice on suitable shoes. The farrier should also study your horse's existing shoes to see how he wears them.

He will then remove the shoes and trim excess horn off the feet. Metal, of course, is malleable when hot and many mobile farriers use a portable forge which enables shoes to be shaped minutely to fit the horse's foot. The hoof should never be chopped about to fit the shoe, although a precise fit is not so easy when the farrier shoes cold, using ready-made shoes which permit only slight adjustment. However, good cold shoeing is very common outside Britain, and racehorses are usually shod that way. Once a mobile farrier gets to know your horse, he should be able to make shoes to fit at his home forge and get a much better fit on his visits.

In hot shoeing, the shoe is pressed very lightly against the horn so that the farrier can see if there is an even burn all round, indicating an even fit. If patches remain unburned, the shoe is corrected on the anvil so that all the bearing surface (ground surface of the hoof wall) comes into contact with the shoe. Uneven contact between shoe and foot creates uneven stresses on the foot and up the leg, resulting in lameness.

The shoe is cooled in water and nailed on; the nail holes should be all the same height unless broken horn prevents it. The ends which protrude through the wall are broken off and bent down (when they are called clenches) to secure the shoe.

Horses' feet differ in their rate of growth, but normally the horn will have grown enough to necessitate removal of the shoes and trimming of the horn in roughly six weeks. If not much worn, the old shoes can be replaced (called 'doing a remove'), but new shoes might be needed.

You can tell if it is time to remove the shoes, trim the feet and reshoe if the horn is growing over the shoe in such a way that the shoe presses into the foot, particularly at the heels, where bruises called corns can be caused; if the horn is cracking; if any of the clenches have risen above their holes, which is highly dangerous because they can rip open the adjacent leg; and if you can hear a clanking sound, indicating a loose shoe, when the horse walks on a hard surface.

Exercise and Fitness

Exercise is probably the one commodity private horses mostly go short of. It is highly unnatural for a horse to stand more or less still in one spot for more than a few minutes, let alone the twenty-two hours or so forced upon stabled horses. Although some experts disagree with turning out fit, working horses, you will find just as many who maintain, as do I, that a daily period out in a paddock for freedom, grass and natural association with other horses does them a world of good. It has a great psychological tonic effect and the grass is a source of mental pleasure apart from being an aid to digestion.

Many horses do not even get the absolute minimum two hours' exercise stipulated for a healthy horse. Their minds and bodies must eventually suffer as a result.

Whatever exercise you can give, it is always better, if at all possible, to split it into two periods a day rather than one, to help break the boredom of standing in. Hopefully, the horse can be turned out for one period and worked for the other.

The type of work your horse gets depends on your environment and facilities. If you are confined to hard roads for your hacking or driving, remember that, despite what often goes on in the hunting field, you should never take a horse at more than a steady (working) trot on hard surfaces. Anyone who genuinely cares about their animal's wellbeing will never trot fast, canter, gallop or jump onto a hard road.

The old riding master I had when I was tiny used to say you should 'walk fast, trot slow and canter in between', and this is, in fact, a good general guide as to exercise paces. The horse should walk smartly, not hurriedly, trot steadily and canter easily unless you are giving him a pipe-opener at a faster pace for fun or for fittening his wind. Out of a two-hour hack or drive, a reasonably fit horse should spend at least an hour of it walking – in general terms, slow work is always beneficial, while fast work rarely is – with most of the rest steady trotting and, for a riding horse, say a couple of canters.

Another old maxim intended to help you warm up your horse

128

gradually and cool him off before arrival home is 'walk the first mile out and the last mile home'. If your horse is the fretful or hyperactive type, it could help to settle him if you dismount and lead him for the last few hundred yards, with stirrups run up and girth let out a hole or two, but not so much that the saddle might slip round.

Getting a horse fit is not a difficult process; it simply requires discipline in yourself to follow a gradually increasing programme of exercise and feeding. A horse which has been holidaying at grass and has become soft and fat should have his grazing time gradually reduced, his concentrate feed gradually increased from nothing, and his exercise stepped up from an initial half hour's daily walking to his normal two hours' walk/trot/canter at the end of six or eight weeks. He should then be half fit – enough for showing, easy showjumping and active hacking and driving, but not enough for driving trials, hunter trials or other cross-country work such as one-day events. For such work, the programme should be continued up to twelve weeks, with faster work and jumping introduced as appropriate. Three-day event horses and racehorses usually have fitness programmes extending to about sixteen weeks.

Letting down the horse from fitness for a rest follows a similar programme in reverse, but nothing like so long. Exercise reduces, as do concentrates, hay/grazing increases and, if the horse is to be turned out, grooming stops to allow some build-up of grease in the coat. Letting down can take about three weeks – the fitter the horse is the longer it takes – because, as in everything, there should be no sudden changes of any kind. If he has been rugged up in winter and you are doing what is called *roughing off* your horse to go out to grass, remember to reduce his clothing gradually, too, otherwise he could feel the cold considerably. Do not be afraid to use a New Zealand rug for his first week or so in the field, until the weather warms up and he becomes acclimatized.

Handling

Kind, confident handling is needed for horses. They are big, strong animals – even a very small pony can easily pull a sixteen-stone man around the stable yard without even feeling it. The expression 'as strong as a horse' wasn't coined for nothing. Your horse must be your friend if you are to have a satisfactory

129

relationship, and in most satisfactory relationships someone is the dominant partner – in this case you must make sure it is you. This does not mean that your horse is never allowed to have his own way, of course. He has a mind and personality of his own, but by and large you are the boss and, when it matters, your horse must obey for the safety of both of you. If he obeys you as a matter of course, should an emergency arise he will obey your instructions instinctively, unless he is really panicking, when primal urges take over both rider and horse.

You must gain and keep the respect of your horse by handling him gently but firmly. Do not forget to speak to him as you approach and move around him. Speak quietly but confidently; do not shout or squeak at him. Do not poke at him nervously with your fingers, but handle him smoothly and firmly, because if you give the impression you are afraid he will react by becoming either afraid, too, or dominant over you.

Remember that he is flesh and blood and the same things that hurt you hurt him, such as thorns in his flesh, bangs on his head or legs, someone poking at open wounds to clean them (so do it gently) or being bitten or kicked by another horse. Ill-fitting tack and rugs can really irritate and even hurt him, as ill-fitting clothes or shoes do you, and he will react in the only way he can – physically – by rubbing or biting at his clothing, flinching under painful tack or harness, or shaking his head at a badly fitting bridle, or unsuitable bit.

The watchwords, then, in horse handling are *calmness, confidence* and *understanding firmness*.

General Safety

This topic is closely related to correct handling, since a horse made insecure by nervous or cruel handling can be a dangerous animal indeed, always on the defensive with teeth and heels and ready to shy or run off at the slightest provocation.

His general environment is important, too, because horses and particularly ponies will always find trouble if the possibility exists. Rugs that have slipped round and are not straightened can be trodden on and the horse can bring himself down. Bandages which have not been properly applied can come undone and trip the horse. Flimsy stables can be kicked and pulled to bits, injuring the horse in the process. Sloppy leading, where the horse is allowed to dawdle along behind you and maybe push you over, is dangerous, as is letting the lead rope trail on the floor for the horse to tread on and bring himself down and maybe you as well.

Always be on the lookout for dangerous situations such as a loose nail protruding in the stable, a loose manger fitment, a broken kicking board for the horse to catch himself on, a haynet too low, a stable door with loose hinges or bolts and anything of a similar nature. In the field, keep a careful watch on the fencing and gates – horses will be sure to find a weak spot or an actual gap. Watch for litter, farm implements, mucking-out tools and other equipment left lying about field, yard or stable. Do not leave empty feed containers lying on the ground, or haynets, or baler twine in the bedding. And remember that polythene bags and sacks can be extremely slippery when trodden on.

Keep a most careful eye on the condition of your tack and harness, watching out for cracking, worn leather and stitching coming undone.

On the roads
When out driving or riding in the vicinity of motorized traffic, follow meticulously the Highway Code (when did you last read it!?) and the advice given in the British Horse Society booklets on safe riding and how to behave in traffic. It is unfortunate that some of the advice given (formulated in conjunction with Police Mounted Branches) in these booklets recommends riders to act in a way opposite to that recommended for cars in the Highway Code, which gives other road users the impression that the horse's rider doesn't know what he or she is doing.

For instance, when turning right we are advised to signal (very clearly) our intentions by means of the usual hand signal (so make sure you can ride with one hand on the reins) and to approach on, and keep to, the *left* of the road up to and beyond the centre of the junction. We should make sure the traffic has given way to us, and then turn sharp right across the road, into the left hand side of the road we wish to take.

This is contrary to the correct procedure for cars, which should pull into the middle of the road (right) and *then* turn.

The idea of the above advice for horse riders is to make sure the horse is not placed in a position where he has traffic on both sides, and be hovering around in the middle of the road waiting for a chance to turn. If the horse *does* panic but has been kept to the left, he can (we hope) be guided up on to the verge or (technically unlawful) the pavement and out of the traffic – not possible when turning as recommended for cars.

The fact remains, however, that the 'horse' way to turn is regarded as incorrect by motorists, not unnaturally, I suppose, and such misunderstanding can cause frayed tempers and a highly fraught situation. The advice for horses at roundabouts is, similarly, keep to the outside (left) when turning right.

I feel the best way to cope is to use the recommended methods for horses, otherwise motorists will never get used to them, but be extra alert, cautious, patient and polite, smiling or in some other way acknowledging that the traffic has given way, then trot *steadily* off in the direction in which you wish to go, keeping your horse under proper control. Above all, *look behind* before making any manoeuvre.

Some of the hand signals used by horse riders can be misunderstood by motorists, too, but full details are given in the British Horse Society booklets mentioned (namely *Ride Safely* and *Responsible Riding*). These are essential reading for horse riders intending to use roads.

It is as well to remember that many motorists consider that horses should not be on the roads and are not averse to giving them and their attendants a fright. Others simply do not think, and consider all horses to be as safe in traffic as police horses. One Mounted Branch I know of always carries out road-training of young horses with riders in civilian riding clothes as they find motorists are more cautious. If they wear uniform, they find, traffic whizzes by a hair's-breadth away assuming that the horse is a trained police mount who won't turn a whisker.

It is best to avoid roads if at all possible, but this is a counsel of perfection in most areas as there are simply not enough bridleways and other riding routes. This should make all riders aware of the dangers of riding on roads, and is reason enough for us all to join and actively participate in our local bridleway groups, whatever our other interests in horses.

If you do go on the roads, always wear a reflective tabard bearing a standard 'Caution' sign to draw motorists' attention to the fact that your horse is a living creature with a mind of his own, and not a motorbike. A similar sign placed on the rear of your vehicle, if driving, should also be used.

If you absolutely must take your horse out in dusk or dark (you must never take a horse out in mist or fog), wear light coloured clothing and a reflective tabard, and a strong stirrup light on your offside stirrup; try to keep to well-lit roads if they are not too busy. If two of you are out together, keep the lightest coloured horse on the outside provided he is sensible in traffic (and if he

132

isn't, train him with the help of a schoolmaster horse, quickly). If the road is narrow, have the light coloured horse at the back – and *both* of you wear lights and reflective equipment.

If driving, make sure your vehicle is well lit and supplied with reflective strips. Such strips are also helpful on the bridle's noseband, and reflective bandages can be obtained for the horse's legs.

Cycling shops also sell useful lights on crossbelts to go over your clothing. Another safety item is a wrist light so that your signals can be seen. It is better to be seen to be a Christmas tree than not to be seen at all!

In short, make sure you are very visible, use the roads correctly, keep your horse under control at all times, be alert, cautious, patient and polite – and you should be a lot safer than many horse riders on the roads today.

When leading a horse where there is likely to be traffic, always lead it in a bridle and bit and maybe a cavesson as well, as this gives strong control. A headcollar or halter is dangerously insufficient as even the best mannered animal can be genuinely frightened.

Road surfaces vary greatly, but most are more or less slippery compared with other footings. It is this feeling of insecure footing which causes many normally calm animals to panic or at least become unsure on roads. To combat this, ask your farrier about tiny 'needle' studs, which are nothing more than an eighth of an inch of borium (or similar hardened material) protruding beyond the ground surface of every heel (inside and outside). These will give your horse enough purchase on the road to restore confidence, and so make panic and loss of control less likely.

In general, always anticipate trouble. You will then be in the best position to overcome it if you meet up with it.

The British Horse Society run riding and road safety tests which are excellent training for you and your horse, and readers are advised to find out about them from the BHS or a BHS-affiliated riding club.

Security

Thefts of both horses and tack are now very common in Britain and it is wise to take as many reasonable precautions as possible to safeguard them. Many stolen horses end up at public auctions and go for meat. Once a horse has passed through the auction ring it can be slaughtered very quickly indeed. Even if the animal is still alive and is traced in time, the law regarding public auctions is such that the rightful owner can only get it back by buying it from the new purchaser. Other horses which 'go missing' are taken by joy-riders and are often discovered miles away in dreadful condition, or released onto public highways exposed to the dangers of traffic.

One of the best deterrents, supported by the police and the British Horse Society, is freeze marking, something I think all owners of horses, ponies and donkeys should do today. The most widespread freeze marking scheme is operated by FarmKey Ltd of Banbury, Oxfordshire, who maintain a register to which the police and British Horse Society have access. Horses are marked by the application of super-cold branding irons bearing an individual number, which apparently does not cause undue discomfort. The cold kills the colouring in the skin, and the hair will regrow white in the shape of your number. For grey horses, the iron is left on a little longer to kill hair growth completely, so that the number is outlined in bare skin. The mark is normally put under the saddle on the left side of the back, so that it is only seen when the horse is untacked. FarmKey offer a substantial reward for the recovery of stolen, freeze-marked animals, and as a result the scheme has been extremely successful. Details are available from FarmKey Ltd, your local police Crime Prevention Department or from the British Horse Society.

As well as having your horse freeze marked, always make sure that gates to your fields and premises are strongly padlocked at both ends, and that they are of the type which cannot be lifted off the hinges. The most secure fencing is thick, prickly hedging, because wire and wooden fences can easily be dismantled by a thief.

Take colour photographs of your horse from back, front and both sides, with close-ups of any distinguishing marks, and have several copies of each print ready to distribute to police, dealers and slaughterhouses. Also contact the Horses and Ponies Protection Association (see Appendix A), who operate a lost-and-found register and can offer advice and help.

Finally, get to know the neighbours near your stable and field. Give them your day and evening telephone numbers and ask them to ring you if any suspicious characters appear.

Tack and harness should be indelibly marked by some police-approved method with your National Insurance number (much more definitive than your postcode, which is what is usually recommended); take photographs of any unusual items. Some saddlers have their own security scheme, and the British Horse Society can also help here. Tack and harness should be kept strongly under lock and key when not in use.

Grassland Care

Unfortunately, many horse owners regard this subject as a bit of a bore. Why bother to look after the field, anyway, they think; the horses will eat whatever grows, anyway, won't they? Well, no, they won't. Horses are fussy grazers and will go hungry rather than eat anything unpleasant to them. They will not, for instance, graze near their own droppings, and, as they designate one area of every field as their loo, this whole area is wasted from a food point of view. They are also rather lazy, doing droppings on the edge of the loo area, which consequently expands with every pile passed.

Research undertaken some years ago by Mrs Marytavy Archer at the Equine Research Station of the Animal Health Trust at Newmarket proved that horses find the smell of equine droppings most objectionable and that, to avoid contamination of the paddock, manure must be picked up within half an hour of being passed – impossible for most of us. She also found, however, that spreading resting paddocks with cattle manure (not pig or poultry manure, which can be dangerous for horses) disguised the smell and made the loo areas available once more for grazing. No manufactured product can achieve this.

However, droppings should still be picked up daily if at all possible, partly because they add to the value of your muck heap, but mainly because removing them prevents contamination of the land by parasite eggs and larvae. A proper worming programme (see the veterinary section, see pages 142–3) helps greatly to reduce the parasite burden, but droppings should still be picked up as a basic pasture management procedure.

Because of horses' selective grazing habits, a paddock which has had horses on it for a few weeks begins to take on a patchy appearance, with some areas grazed very short and others growing longer and practically untouched. If this is allowed to continue, the overgrazed areas will become as bare as a billiard table and the others will become rank and coarse. The paddock should therefore be rested and, if at all possible, cattle put on it to drop their manure on the horses' overgrazed areas. These areas are too short for the cattle to graze, because they pull up grass with their tongues; on the other hand they will eat off the long grass spurned by the horses, including that in the loo areas. After the cattle have gone, after about two or three weeks, and in any case if you cannot get hold of any, remaining long grass should be cut and the paddock thoroughly harrowed, then left to grow to about 4–6 inches (15–20cm) before reinstating the horses. The paddock they have been using during this time should now be given the same treatment, and so on.

The paddocks should be liberally spread with cattle manure in early spring and late autumn. Although in some areas this is difficult to get, every effort should be made to do so as it is an excellent organic fertilizer and, as mentioned above, a smell disguiser for horse paddocks. You can hardly go wrong with it.

The above is an oversimplified version of grassland management and use on a rota system but is, nevertheless, the minimum care you should give paddocks; sadly, it is more than most get. Soil analysis should really be carried out periodically, and other fertilizers applied according to the results. Fertilizer firms can do this for you, but many are quite ignorant of horses' requirements, which are different from those of cattle. Too much quick-acting nitrogen, for example, can be disastrous for horses. Firms are also naturally biased towards their own products, so to get independent advice you need to contact a similarly independent consultant, such as the Equine Management Consultancy Service (see Appendix A) or other expert.

A word about using your own stable muck on your paddocks: although fresh droppings are known to make the surrounding grass unacceptable to horses, it is thought that old, thoroughly rotted ones do not, and several horse owners have told me that their horses grazed freely and happily on sections of their paddocks previously spread with their own well-rotted manure. It should be about a year old, apparently, and is of course free, unlike all other products.

Haymaking
Many large and medium-sized establishments shut up their paddocks to grow a hay crop in the spring. The grass then has to grow again, so it is early autumn or late summer before the land is free for grazing by horses. This understandably infuriates the livery clients, because their horses' grazing can be drastically cut or even eliminated at a time of year when they should be enjoying freedom, grass and the sun on their backs.

136

The practice is, in fact, of little value in many cases because such paddocks often do not receive good care and the resulting hay crop can be mediocre and often useless. The proprietors think they are saving money, but hay of this kind can have low feeding value, so more has to be fed, or more expensive concentrates given, to maintain the horses in good condition; so it is not economical after all.

If an establishment follows this procedure it should reserve at least some land for the horses at this prime time of year. The economics of the situation can be as broad as they are long, anyway, as horses on grass consume less other food, so for the most part it is not worth doing. Your stable cannot expect you to pay a grazing fee during these times, so take account of this, and if the situation becomes unpleasant and you are denied grazing for your horse, look around for another place.

Veterinary Matters

All horse owners should have a knowledge of veterinary care and are strongly advised to buy at least one good book on the subject (see Appendix B). Here are the basics to start you off.

Signs of health and disease
Before you can begin to assess what is wrong with your horse, if anything, you need to know what is right! In other words, you must know what he is like when he is healthy and normal before you can hope to know what is abnormal for him.

A healthy horse has a smooth, glossy coat which moves easily when you push it with the flat of your hand, usually over the ribs. He has bright eyes, an interested expression and is curious about his environment; the mucous membranes inside his eyelids and nostrils and his gums should be salmon pink, not pale, yellowish, bluish or an angry red, all of which indicate disorder. He should have a general air of wellbeing and, depending on his normal temperament, a zest for life.

Even if your horse lives out, when he will always be more or less dirty, his coat should be bright-looking and supple. If it is dull and lifeless, and if it feels stiff, or if it 'stares' (stands away from his skin), something could be wrong.

Other signs of disorder are dull, perhaps sunken eyes, listlessness, keeping away from other horses and standing with his head down looking dejected. Lack of appetite is a sign of illness,

137

although in hard-working horses on high-concentrate diets, lack of appetite can indicate indigestion – not exactly an illness, but still something amiss. Lying down a lot, and for more than half an hour at a time, particularly during the day, is another pointer to illness. The horse could also have a general air of being out of sorts.

It is easy to take for granted a horse you know well. Make a point of checking every day, usually when you first see him, that he appears normal. Often, your first impression on any particular day is correct. If you get the feeling – as you may well when you have owned your horse for a while – that something is not right, don't dismiss it as your imagination. Although you may not be as expert as the owner and staff at your yard, he is your horse and no one else can possibly develop the rapport with him that you have if you are a conscientious, loving owner. No one else has the time, and they have many other horses to care for. So if you suspect all is not well, discuss matters with the stable staff and send for the vet if appropriate.

Temperature, pulse and respiration
In addition to following your hunch and generally looking over the horse, there are three closely linked guidelines to well-being: they are your horse's temperature, pulse and respiration rates. These can help you assess physical fitness in conditioning programmes, but they are also valuable checks on general health.

Every owner should know his or her horse or pony's normal rates, so that you have some definite clinical information to give the yard proprietor and vet when necessary; then they will know you are not worrying needlessly, and so will you. Often, a minor change in these rates can herald the onset of some disorder before any other signs are visible. A well-used phrase in veterinary terminology and one which most owners seem not to understand is *subclinical disease*. A horse suffering from a subclinical disease is one which is so mildly ill that the symptoms are not outwardly present or are so slight that they escape the notice of the horse's attendants. However, if you take the TPR (temperature, pulse and respiration) rates of such a horse, one of them is very often abnormal for that particular animal.

It takes no more than five minutes to take all three rates and they are all easy to check. All are lower in a fit horse than in an unfit, but healthy, one, and all three increase after exercise, although there is not scope here to describe their use in assessing fitness. If possible, the rates should be taken every day – although very few people actually do so – and at the same time and under the same conditions every day; even in a resting horse they vary during the day. Average rates are as follows:

Temperature   38°C (100·4°F)

Pulse   36–42 beats per minute

Respiration   8–14 breaths per minute (in and out counting as one)

In small animals the last two rates will be slightly higher. These rates, however, are only average for horses in general. They may by no means be the averages for your particular horse, so take them every day for a week to discover whether he is above or below these general averages. If, for instance, your vet reads the horse's temperature as 38°C he might take that to be normal; but if your horse's personal normal is known to be, say, 36·5°C or 39°C, there is in fact a discrepancy. This could throw the vet off the track if no other symptoms are present, and valuable time might be lost.

To take temperature, use the thermometer from your first aid kit and shake the mercury down below 32°C (90°F) before use, as you will have seen your doctor do many times. Moisten or grease the bulb with Vaseline or spit and, standing to one side of the quarters, hold the dock towards you with your free hand. Gently insert the thermometer into the anus with a gentle side-to-side twisting movement, and tilt it a little so it touches the side of the rectum rather than going into a ball of dung where the temperature will be a little lower. Push the thermometer in but keep hold of the top, and leave it in as long as the directions say – there are half-minute and one-minute types. Gently pull it out, wipe it on the horse's tail and read off the figure where the mercury is.

To take pulse, use your fingers at any point where an artery crosses a bone, commonly under the jawbone (where the round part meets the straight one), above the eye, inside the elbow a little way down, under the dock or at the side of the dock about a third of the way down. Feel around with your fingers till you are sure you have a pulse and count for half a minute, timing yourself with a watch that has a second hand. Double your count and that's his rate.

To take respiration, stand behind and just to one side of the horse and count the rise and fall of his flank on the side farthest from you, each rise and fall being one breath. Again, use your watch. It can be difficult to spot respiration in a very fit horse, in which

139

case hold a mirror up to his nostrils and note how often it steams up!

Some common illnesses and situations

Lameness is a curse present at some time or other in all horses. Most of it occurs in the foot and fetlock area, decreasing as one passes up the leg. The famous and much-heard-of shoulder lameness is, in practice, quite rare. If a horse is lame he will naturally throw his weight off the leg that hurts onto the sound one. If lame in front he will take a shorter step with the lame leg, drop his weight down onto the sound one and drop his head lower on that leg, too. If lame behind, the same thing applies, and the hock and hip of the lame leg will appear to be higher than those on the sound leg.

To test for lameness always trot up the horse on a hard, level surface. Trot in a circle to right and left as well as in a straight line, because work on a circle shows up even very slight lameness which might not be spotted on a straight line.

Your farrier should always trot up your horse or pony after shoeing to check that no nails have been driven too near, or even into, the sensitive interior of the foot.

Heat and swelling in foot or leg are useful signs that there is either infection or injury present, such as a strain. Use the backs of your fingers (more sensitive than the inside of your hand) to gauge heat; feel first what you believe to be the sound leg, then you can compare the suspect one and detect any change in temperature.

Wounds can be of varying types and will be detailed in any good veterinary book. Never delay in cleaning a wound, otherwise you could be faced with an infection as well. If more than the top layer of skin is damaged, the wound will probably need stitching – a job for your vet.

Colic (indigestion, severe or otherwise) is probably the most frightening condition you may have to face. A horse with colic can throw itself around most violently and become dangerous. Colic just means abdominal pain and can range from mild indigestion to a twisted or ruptured intestine. The horse may have a wild, frightened look on his face, show patchy sweating, paw the ground, look round and try to bite his flanks, lie down and try to roll and maybe kick out violently and plunge about. If he is violent, keep out of his way for safety's sake, but you must always call the vet immediately, even in the middle of the night, because colic in horses can easily be fatal.

140

Laminitis is a painful condition caused by faulty blood supply to the feet due to too many poisons circulating in the blood. Often it results from overfeeding, but it can occur in blood poisoning and other conditions.

The horse's hoof is lined inside the wall with horny leaves running from top to bottom, which interlock with sensitive, fleshy leaves covering the bones of the foot. This system keeps the bones in place, but in laminitis the sensitive leaves (known as the sensitive laminae) become inflamed and can come away from the insensitive, horny ones. The pedal bone of the foot, which gives it its shape, can then rotate downwards and press on the sensitive sole inside the foot near the toe, sometimes causing a visibly lowered or dropped horny sole.

The horse naturally wishes to avoid the severe pain and stands with his weight on his heels, leaning backwards, and will be most reluctant to move. He may well lie down, when it will be very difficult to get him up again. Again, he will look highly distressed and may show patchy sweating. If he waves a foot in the air it is a sign of great pain, whether he has laminitis or something else.

The horse must be put where he cannot eat anything, so if he is out he will have to come in and be put on inedible bedding but with a constant supply of water. Again, call the vet immediately.

Tying-up syndrome, often called *azoturia*, is also caused by faulty management and usually occurs in fit horses who have been kept cooped up during their day off without their concentrates being reduced or cut out, as they should be. On resuming exercise the horse soon seizes up and staggers, eventually refusing to move – movement would in fact cause severe muscle damage in the hardened, cramp-afflicted muscles of back and quarters.

If you are out on a hack or drive you may have no choice but to try to get the horse home at a gentle walk (he will not have come too far anyway); if a cooperative passer-by happens along, ask him or her to ring your yard and/or vet. The horse must have veterinary attention as soon as possible.

Filled legs and *lymphangitis* are two similar conditions also caused by faulty feeding and management – largely overfeeding plus sluggish circulation with lack of exercise. Some horses fill in the legs (usually the hind) all the time, but true lymphangitis often occurs in one leg only, which will be as hard as a marble column and similar in shape. Discuss continual filled legs with your yard owner, but get the vet for lymphangitis. Rubbing with liniments and hosing with cold water is a waste of time and money.

141

Influenza can be very serious in horses and can leave them with permanently impaired, or at least sensitive, respiratory systems. The horse will be listless and miserable, with a watery discharge from the nostrils and a raised temperature. He may or may not be coughing. Keep him in a well-ventilated box but well rugged up and call the vet at once.

Coughing is as much of a bugbear to horse owners as lameness, because it has so many causes. It can mean next to nothing or it can herald a serious disorder or a troublesome, incapacitating allergy. Some horses will have a cough and a splutter on first starting exercise just to clear their wind, especially if they have been stabled, but if it does not subside after five or ten minutes discontinue exercise, take the horse's temperature and call the vet.

From reading the above short list of some of the most common disorders you may have received the impression that life is going to be one long telephone call to the vet. Actually, there are many first aid situations you will learn to deal with yourself, but the fact remains that your vet is highly important and you should budget for his or her services so that you need never hesitate to call in professional help when it is needed.

Your vet can also assist you in formulating a yearly health plan to help keep your horse in good order. This will probably comprise an annual medical, probably before your most energetic, active season starts, and may involve blood tests to monitor general health as well as other investigations as necessary.

Vaccinations will be needed to protect your horse or pony against influenza and tetanus. You should have asked his previous owner for his current vaccination certificates or at least for information on what vaccinations he has received, so that you can inform your vet. If you do not know, tell the vet and he or she will decide what to do. Boosters will be needed every so often, and your vet will work out a suitable programme for them.

Worms can cause considerable problems in horses, who pick up the larvae of these parasites (there are several types) from the pasture when grazing and swallow them; the larvae migrate around inside the horse's body via the blood vessels. They can cause aneurisms (ballooned and blocked arteries) and also severe damage to the intestines when they mature and return there to mate and lay eggs which are passed out in the droppings, so recommencing the cycle. The most dangerous worms are red-

142

worms (*Strongylus vulgaris*) but there are others. Just because you cannot see the worms in the droppings it does not mean that your horse has none, as some worms are very small and their eggs and larvae microscopic.

Bots, another parasite, are not worms but the larvae of the botfly, which lays its eggs on the horse's body. The horse licks them off and the larvae congregate in the stomach, causing damage to the stomach wall and also colic.

Your veterinary surgeon may do an egg count from a sample of your horse's droppings. However many assume – often safely so – that the horse will be infested, and simply supply a broad-spectrum (wide-ranging) anthelmintic (worm medicine), to be given as pellets, or as powder in the feed, or as paste. You squirt the paste from a plastic syringe, inserted in the corner of your horse's mouth, onto the back of his tongue – he will usually swallow the paste.

Worm medicines have to be given every four to eight weeks, depending on the number of horses in your paddocks and the management. Medicines will have to be given more frequently to animals kept in relatively crowded conditions in paddocks which never have the droppings picked up than to those on generous acreages where droppings are picked up regularly. On a regular basis, one horse per 2 acres of land is quite enough. I know one grassland consultant who advises that each 10 acres should carry ten cows and one horse, as horses spoil pasture whereas cows are good for it. This is the reason why many farmers will not let out their land for horses.

Your vet will confirm that the only effective way of keeping horses as worm-free as practicable is to worm all the horses at an establishment regularly and at the same time. The medicines kill the adult worms in the intestine (and at least one wormer now available kills the migrating larvae), and so severely incapacitate those few that are left that their mating and egg-laying activities are hampered for several weeks. It will take this long for the immature population to reach the intestine and become mature enough to mate, but by then you will be giving another dose, so dealing this lot a body blow, too, and so on. Eventually, this kind of programme results in paddocks and horses as worm-free as we can hope for under domestication, but a little neglect can easily reverse the process.

9. Activities to Enjoy

When you were first thinking of buying your horse you probably had some idea of the type of equestrian disciplines you wanted to take part in. People often find, however, that once they get into the swing of horse ownership they change their minds and move in a different direction. They also discover other activities which they did not even know existed, so this short chapter is aimed at giving details of some of the things you might wish to do with your horse.

First, there is of course no obligation on you to do anything competitive at all. Despite the impression you might get from reading various horse magazines, life does exist outside the competitive field and not everyone wants to pit their skills and talents and those of their horse against others. The pressure even of local show competition is anathema to many people who simply wish to enjoy a horse for his own sake. There is nothing wrong, indeed everything to be gained, by improving your abilities in dressage or jumping just for your own fulfilment.

Hacking is a wonderful way of getting to know both your horse and the area surrounding his stable yard. Seeing the countryside from the back of a horse is most enjoyable and relaxing, provided your area is suitable and the traffic is not too heavy for hacking out. There are bridleways all over the country crying out for people like you to open them up, keep them open and so help keep horses off busy roads.

Joining a bridleways group (contact the British Horse Society for details of your nearest group) gives you support in cases where you find a right of way blocked or impassable, and although ill feeling can arise between landowners and farmers and people who wish to use these paths, the fact remains that they are rights of way and it is your right to use them free of hindrance.

You will learn about the Country Code in a bridleway group because following it is an essential part of being a responsible citizen. Farmers do have legitimate grudges against people who charge off across farmland, damaging crops and disturbing stock, not to mention leaving gates open, and this irresponsible minority spoils it for the rest.

Hacking or driving on bridleways is a lot safer and more pleasant than using hard roads, and you can use them to give your horse his canters. Some of my happiest days have been spent on horseback exploring bridleways, discovering old ones and getting them opened up for the benefit of myself and other horse owners. If you behave responsibly and pleasantly to other people you may become known and trusted, and could, as I have been, be granted special privileges such as riding across private land or on tracks which are not public rights of way.

You do not have to join a bridleways group, of course, to use rights of way, but if you have the formal support of like-minded people, in a group which is probably affiliated to the British Horse Society, you will find it so much simpler when you encounter difficulties over blocked paths.

If you are fortunate enough to live in an area with open spaces on which you can ride, such as moors, beaches, downs, forests and the like, your hacking will be that much more enjoyable. Make the most of it.

Hunting is another equestrian sport which is non-competitive. It can be very expensive, depending on where you hunt, but no one will make you feel guilty for letting the side down if you don't wish to turn out, if you fall off, if you forget the course or if your horse refuses. You might, however, receive a dressing down if you or your horse forget your manners!

Riding clubs are where most first-time owners get their introduction to competition, and they can be very competitive indeed between individual members, on a regional inter-club basis, and up to national level. Even if you eventually decide that the riding club scene is not for you, you will learn a lot of basic information within the riding club movement, gain experience and probably make many friends and acquaintances with similar interests. Clubs normally run regular instruction classes, shows, hunter trials, one-day events and showjumping and dressage events of varying standards, from beginners upwards. You will

145

be exposed to the whole gamut of activities and can develop your interests accordingly.

The club environment will also expose the strengths and weaknesses of both you and your horse, and you might change your aspirations accordingly. For instance, you might find that you have a superb jumper on your hands yet you yourself daren't jump a stick, or you might want to do dressage but your horse has other ideas and prefers hunter trials. You will be able to discover what you can both do or cannot do, maybe after some instruction, advice and experience.

Remember, horses and ponies do change after a while in new hands, sometimes for the better and sometimes for the worse, but a riding club will certainly give you a chance to try your hand at everything.

Driving clubs are not quite so numerous as riding clubs but the majority of areas are well enough supplied with them. Most organize regular forays into the surrounding district and hold shows and instructional rallies. They can also introduce you to driving trials, an increasingly popular and publicized sport. Many people take up driving when they cannot bear to part with their children's much-loved family pony, who is then pressed into service between the shafts to entertain the adult members of the family.

Showjumping is the most famous equestrian sport because of its exposure on television and the fact that it is convenient to stage at shows. On a national scale, the lowest standard is Foxhunter, but even that can be quite overwhelming to anyone only used to riding club classes. It certainly makes you see international riders in a highly respectful light! You obviously need a horse with real jumping ability for this sport to make the height and spread of even Grade C classes (the next up from Foxhunter) – as a matter of interest, I have heard three-day event riders say they have been frightened by the sheer size of the fences in Grade B classes, and one told me she would not enter a Grade A class to save her life.

Few riders make this standard, however, and you can certainly enjoy showjumping at riding club level or just above without having to frighten yourself out of your wits – provided you have a horse with jumping ability.

Hunter trials also demand jumping ability, but as these are purely cross-country jumping competitions you will not normally be faced with excessive heights as in showjumping. However your horse needs the ability to gallop on if you want to be in the ribbons – though there is no reason why you shouldn't enter just for the fun of the ride.

In hunter trials you compete alone, so it is not a true representation of hunting, from which it takes its name. However, in *team chasing* teams of four go round together, so if your horse will not jump in cold blood the company of the others might encourage him. The standard is usually high and the pace fast, so you and your horse need to be quite competent before making the team.

Eventing, sometimes called *horse trials*, is a sport needing an equine all-rounder, as dressage, showjumping (fairly low fences!) and cross-country are all involved. In two- and three-day events the standard and demands made on the horse are quite high, and there is a steeplechase course which you must take alone at racing pace – not an activity for the novice. However, one-day events are run at various levels and you will probably get experience first in riding club events, so if your horse has the obedience, presence and action for dressage (plus the necessary calm and cooperative temperament), the precision for showjumping and the speed and courage for cross-country, you could well find that eventing is your sport.

If you decide that jumping of any kind is not for you, there are still some suitable competitive sports. If your horse is good-looking and has presence, *showing* could be his métier. A show class is really a beauty competition, so blemishes such as lumps, bumps and scars usually count you out unless your horse looks superb in other respects and gives the judge a good ride. You must be sure to enter the right class for his type (see Chapter 1) or you could be sent out of the ring. For horses who do not fit into a standard category of type, many shows have Riding Horse classes, which cover a multitude of sins and virtues, and also Working Hunter classes; however you do have to jump in these events.

If your horse is no oil painting or lacks the other attributes of the conventional show horse, try entering Equitation or Best Rider classes where it is you and your riding ability which are judged, rather than your horse. Even if your horse behaves badly, the judge will – or should – be looking for your ability to get the best from it.

But what if even these are not what you want? At many riding club and smaller shows there are Best Turned Out and Neatest and Cleanest classes. Here, all that is judged is the cleanliness and turn-out of you and your horse. Your tack and clothing need not be expensive or highly fashionable, but must be in excellent order, clean, correctly fitted and appropriate (i.e. no anoraks but a tweed or show jacket, no red nylon web bridles but a suitable leather one). You can also improve your horse's appearance by producing immaculate plaits and sharp quarter, flank or shoulder marks. Anything which shows that you have taken trouble to make your horse and yourself look clean and tastefully turned out will help you win.

Dressage is another discipline which can be extremely competitive but in which there is no jumping, except in Prix Caprilli classes where cavalletti or tiny jumps are used. Showing does, in fact, involve endless waiting about in the line for your turn to come which bores many horses, who then do not produce their best show when called. With dressage there is none of this. You can time your programme on the day to your allotted schedule and keep your horse interested meanwhile.

Learning a dressage test is only like learning a dance routine or a poem, and the judge does not ride your horse as in many show classes. Because of this, if you know your horse well and are good at acting you can pull off a superb-looking test while your horse is, in reality, pulling like a train or having a raging argument with you, and the judge will never know! The audience at a demonstration given by one of Britain's Olympic dressage riders was amused to hear her say that it is useful to cultivate a pleasant half smile for use during your tests so that you look calm and happy but can swear at your horse, or at least give him verbal instructions under your breath and between your teeth (strictly against the rules) to help produce results without anyone knowing!

Long-distance or endurance riding is another equestrian activity where no jumping of any significance is required, although a willingness to pop over ditches and small treetrunks is useful. Here you compete against yourself rather than other people, except in the 100-mile-in-one-day races, where the outright winner is the first across the finishing line in good condition.

Rides such as the British Horse Society's Golden Horseshoe, for example, regularly produce several equal awards to competitors ending up with the right number of marks for a certain category. Some of the easier rides (from 5 to 25 miles usually) are called *Competitive Trail Rides* and these are well within the reach of any normally active riding horse. Many a hunter covers much more than this in a day with hounds.

The object of most rides is to complete the course with your horse (never mind the rider!) in a fit condition to continue without harm to himself. You are awarded condition marks (for fitness and wellbeing) and veterinary marks (for fitness, again, and also injuries, or rather lack of them), and it is in this respect that you compete against yourself by producing your best possible horsemastership. Obviously a poor, unbalanced rider will adversely affect his or her horse or pony's chances, so reasonable riding ability also comes into it if you are not to tire your animal needlessly.

You need a fit, sound, sensible horse for this sport, who also needs to be a bit of a goer – in other words not lazy. Although good conformation helps produce good, economical action, your horse can in theory be built like a camel as long as he can cover the miles. He does not need to be fast, either, because, as already stated, it is those finishing in good condition who win awards.

Three other equestrian sports which are highly specialized but not out of reach for many are *polo, racing* (including amateur *point-to-pointing*) and *harness racing or trotting*.

Polo is very much a team event, of course, but unless you can borrow friends' ponies (polo animals are always called ponies despite their type and height) or are good enough to have animals loaned to you to enable you to be in the team, it is hardly a sport for the first-time owner because you need a string of ponies rather than just one. This is obviously too expensive for most riders, although the Pony Club does now run polo for its members.

Racing, at least flat racing, is out of reach for many unless they are small, light and have the grit and determination to become a professional in a trainer's yard. Most trainers take on young lads as apprentices, in fact, and it is extremely difficult to break into flat racing in any other way.

Steeplechasing demands tough, fearless riders, but amateurs can obtain licences to ride against professionals if they prove their fitness and ability. It is an extremely dangerous sport, and its relative, *hurdling*, is only slightly less so, but a similar sport strictly for amateurs only is point-to-pointing. This is run by various hunts in the country and you have to qualify your horse for 'pointing' by hunting in the early part of the season. Most people do not take their horses out after Christmas as the season starts in February and the risk of injury in the hunting field is considered too great.

10. Transportation

Very few horses these days go through life without having to be transported at some time or other. It is one aspect of horse management which can cause a great deal of trouble, which is why it has been given a short chapter of its own.

The reason why many horses are bad travellers is that they have at some time been hurt or frightened, or at least made extremely uncomfortable, during a journey. For a start, a trailer or horsebox is an extremely unnatural environment. Very often the horses cannot even see out, and the motion of the vehicle must feel most strange to them. Problems occur because animals will not enter the vehicle or because they play up once inside, whether it is moving or not, and a few are simply claustrophobic. Many problems, however, are caused by bad driving. Either the driver goes too fast, causing the vehicle to sway alarmingly, or is careless about bumps and holes in the road, which cause a terrifying bang and jar to the occupants in the back. Fast cornering, causing the vehicle to tilt, is also a sure way to unbalance and frighten a horse, as is too-sharp braking.

Many problems would be resolved if drivers would only imagine they had a glass of fine wine balanced on the bonnet or dashboard of their car or horsebox, and that to spill a single drop would be a sacrilege! This is the kind of driving needed when transporting horses.

Another major cause of transport problems is that horses are, by convention and tradition, usually made to ride in an unnaturally stressful and unbalanced way, facing the direction of travel. Scientific and practical evidence is now available which

150

shows that horses travel most easily, and therefore happily, with their tails to the engine.

The horse is so built that he carries about two-thirds of his weight in his forehand and one-third in his quarters. When he stands facing the engine, therefore, the weight is forced back onto his quarters by the momentum of travel, causing stress and strain in an area not meant to bear so much weight. This causes extreme discomfort, even pain, and anxiety. The horse uses his head and neck to balance himself in the same way as we use our arms. Forced to brace his quarters and back to bear the weight thrust upon them, the horse cannot carry his head and neck naturally and so cannot use them to balance himself properly. In addition, when the vehicle brakes, the horse's weight is thrown more or less suddenly forward again, and the horse can be in fear of knocking his head. With his quarters to the direction of travel, no such fear exists.

If you travel a horse loose in a horsebox with no partitions, he will probably position himself with his tail to the engine, maybe diagonally with his tail in a corner, but almost never with his head facing the direction of travel. This must surely tell us something!

Unfortunately, in Britain at least, it is almost impossible to find a trailer which permits the horses to travel in a balanced manner with tails to the engine. Some horseboxes allow this, and some travel horses sideways, which seems at least less stressful to them than facing forwards. It is true that many horses show no outward distress when facing forward, but their pulse rate will normally be abnormally high, indicating at least apprehension about the journey to come.

Many professional trainers acknowledge that travelling takes a good deal out of their horses, so surely we should do what we can to make journeys as stress-free as possible (a) by travelling them tail to the engine whenever possible and (b) by driving carefully and smoothly. When purchasing your own transport always try to buy a trailer or box which permits balanced travel, but do not convert a forward-facing trailer for rear-facing travel as the position of the axles and towbar have normally been designed to ensure level balance and nose weight when horses are facing forward with most of their weight on their forehands and so in the front half of the trailer. If the trailer were redesigned internally to take the horses the other way round, but the axles and towbar not also adjusted, the horses' weight would be mainly in the rear half of the trailer which would tip it and the car out of balance and produce a very dangerous outfit.

151

If you rely on contractors or friends to take your horse about, try to ensure a rear-facing position for him whenever possible and, if you want your horse to be a good traveller for life, tactfully impress on the driver that you would be most grateful if, for the sake of your horse, he or she would be extremely careful not to spill that glass of vintage wine!

Horseboxes, trailers and cattle wagons

Horseboxes undoubtedly give a more stable ride (driver permitting) than trailers, which are prone to jack-knifing when carelessly driven, but cost more in road tax and insurance. Cattle wagons are highly unsuitable for transporting horses (or cattle come to that) as there are no solid partitions for protection – just wooden or metal bars which do nothing to prevent animals treading on each other, particularly if one loses its footing. If you care about your horse or pony, avoid going to an event rather than take him in a cattle wagon.

Laws and insurance

It is illegal for a private owner to transport other people's animals for hire or reward, although it is very common. Professional transporters also have adequate insurance to cover your animal (or should have), but your friends and acquaintances might not; if there is an accident of any kind, whether their fault or not, they are in trouble and you cannot get compensation. Do, therefore, be most careful whom you allow to transport your precious horse.

If you rent a vehicle or trailer, check on the insurance situation; you will probably have to arrange your own for the occasion. If you decide to buy your own trailer, again check on the insurance situation, and if you are going to be doing much travelling, consider buying a small horsebox (you will not need a heavy goods vehicle licence if its unladen weight is less than 3 tons) rather than a trailer. Despite the extra expense – though you need only tax and, depending on your company, insure, it on a seasonal basis if that is all you require – you will find the extra stability and convenience it offers well worthwhile.

Horses with problems

As mentioned, many problems occur when horses are carelessly driven, so it is best, by ensuring good driving, not to let trouble start. However, if a horse does become difficult to transport or you buy one whom you know to be difficult, you should first do

152

all you can to ensure he is as comfortable as possible in transit. Some horses like a lot of room, others prefer a narrow partition, and all horses must have plenty of room in front of their noses so that they are not standing cramped up and cannot possibly hit their heads, if travelling forwards, during braking. A sturdy breastbar in addition to plenty of space will help here.

When loading, face the entrance uphill, if possible, so that the horse does not have to clamber up an unnecessarily steep ramp, and do not use a vehicle which has a space between ramp and container large enough for a horse to get its foot in. Also make sure that the sun or other light is shining into it, so that it does not look like a dark, gaping cavern. Straw on the floor and ramp helps to provide familiar footing.

Feeding animals inside helps to familiarize them with the vehicle, and they come to associate it with something pleasant. Also, loading them and unloading them without actually going anywhere helps get them used to things, and short 'mock' trips round the block lets them realize there is not always an exciting occasion at the other end.

If your horse or pony refuses to enter the box and he absolutely has to (perhaps in order to get home again!) try tempting him in with a bucket of food, or use the old trick of fastening two ropes or lunge lines, one to each side of the opening, and crossing them behind his quarters while gradually tightening them and so winching him in; this usually works. If it doesn't, you could try giving him a sharp scrub under the tail with a stiff stable broom, if there's one handy, or with a handful of brushwood – often most effective!

If these measures fail, you will have to call in expert help and advice. Sometimes it is simply a question of the horse needing a little time to make up his mind or pluck up courage. It can be a very difficult situation but, whatever happens, never let anyone thrash your horse into going in the vehicle. It usually doesn't work and is a certain way of souring him for life; you could not blame him for refusing to go near a trailer or horsebox again after such treatment, as he will probably associate them with a beating for the rest of his life. Horses have elephantine memories!

It is worth mentioning that some people make their own horses hard to load by their indecisive, doubtful attitude. If you firmly fix it in your mind that your horse is going up that ramp, up he may well go. Perhaps he simply needs someone to put his forefoot on the ramp to show him it won't bite it off. Be calm, unhurried and

153

determined in your own mind, and you are unlikely to create a difficult traveller.

Preparation for a journey
You should load everything you need into your vehicle first; the horse goes in last. Protective clothing such as a rug or light sheet (depending on the weather), a poll-guard attached to the head-collar, knee and hock boots plus stable bandages over padding (or special travel boots) and a tail bandage or guard are usually worn. Take a full haynet for the return journey, and for the first half of the outward journey if it is a long one, probably a feed for your horse at the event and a camping container of drinking water. As well as your tack, harness or other gear, remember your first aid kit.

On arrival, if it is hot remember that your horse will suffer considerably if he is kept in the vehicle, particularly if it is not possible to park in the shade, so someone should be available to lead him about or stand with him in sheltered conditions, as appropriate.

Finally, don't tie the horse up short in the vehicle – remember he needs to balance with his head and neck.

11. Moving On

There may come a time when you realize that your present horse, much as you love him, does not have the abilities or scope to take you further up the ladder of success, if you are competitively minded. On the other hand, your domestic or financial circumstances may change for the worse for reasons quite outside your control, and you might find you can no longer keep a horse.

The situation of having to part with a loved horse or pony can be extremely unpleasant as you will naturally be worried about his future home. If this is the case, why not try leasing or lending him to a good home which gives you the opportunity to take him back, if temporarily, should you find he is not being looked after properly? You must discuss the terms with a solicitor, but this could well be the answer to your problems. You might find someone who could give him a super home but simply hasn't the cash sum to actually buy a horse, and in such cases leasing can be ideal.

If you need money and have to sell him, or cannot for some reason lease him, please, above all, do your best to get him a good home, preferably with someone known or recommended to you, and visit it first to gauge the condition of their other animals, if any, or those at the place where he will be kept. This is by no means unreasonable, and anyone fit to own a living creature will not object to such a visit.

Remember that if you sell your horse through a public auction, you have absolutely no say at all where he goes – and he will probably go for meat unless you take special care to put an above-meat price reserve on him. You can use the same sources of supply as you investigated when buying him and, as long as he is yours, you can stipulate where he goes, even to a dealer and particularly to an agency – but get everything in writing first so that you can claim the horse back should your conditions not be met.

Unfortunately, legal actions can be expensive and time-consuming. Simply remember that so long as the horse is legally yours, you have full rights in law over him. The instant he legally belongs to someone else, except where certain conditions of sale have been laid down, you lose those rights and your control over his destiny. This is why leasing a loved animal is such a good idea if you can arrange it.

Your new horse

You are now, of course, an experienced owner. You have gone through the mill of finding, examining and buying, not to mention keeping, a horse and will have learned a good deal in the process. Therefore, buying your second horse will not be unfamiliar ground.

If you are progressing to keeping a horse at home, remember that he is likely to need company, and this might be a good excuse for keeping your first horse as well! If your first animal was a pony and you need a larger horse, perhaps the pony (maybe outgrown by your children) can be kept and turned to driving, as mentioned earlier.

If you are moving on from, say, a hardy cob-type animal to something more breedy, remember that the new animal will be more difficult to keep. He will be more sensitive to the weather and will probably need stabling more than his predecessor, which is expensive in terms of both time and money. If you are intending to compete more, this in itself will cost more money in fees, not to mention transport costs. Your new horse will probably need more food than your first, so this involves more expense again.

If, after considering all this, you still want a Number Two and successfully acquire one, you will be in the position of forming a new relationship all over again with a quite different personality, a quite different ride or drive and probably a quite different-looking animal. This will broaden your expertise and outlook, but try not to compare the two with each other too much. They are both individuals with a right to be different!

Even with your second horse, be careful not to overhorse yourself even though you may naturally want more of a challenge. The right horse for you will still have to be found if you wish to continue to enjoy horse ownership or achieve any success in competition. Your Number Two will depend on you every bit as much as Number One did, so it is unfair to him as well as to yourself to buy an animal with which you cannot cope either physically or mentally.

If you find, with any horse, that you do not get on, that you cannot, after all, afford the time or money to keep him properly, or that the pressures and responsibilities of actual ownership are more than you bargained for, for goodness sake do not hang onto your horse and neglect him. Pass him onto someone who can care for him in the manner which he deserves.

Horse ownership is meant to be enjoyable – most of the time, anyway – and, even though you may have to keep your horse, or horses, on premises other than your own, it will give you quite a thrill to be told by staff or other owners that it is only when your horse hears your particular car coming down the road, or your particular voice in the yard, that he kicks his stable door or comes to the gate and nickers in anticipation of your company, even when you have not seen him for several days. It is a wonderfully warming feeling which makes all the time, money and, yes, occasional worry well worthwhile.

Appendix A
Organizations and Societies

People new to horse or pony ownership will probably be able to gain a good deal of help and support, not to mention interest and new friends, by joining one or more equestrian organizations, depending on their particular interests in the horse world. The organizations marked with an asterisk below are suitable for public membership (some are professional organizations) and will be pleased to send their literature to you. Many organize their own shows and events, particularly the breed societies, and it could be said that *all* horse owners should, as a matter of principle, join the British Horse Society, even if only for the possibly mercenary reason of acquiring free third-party insurance! Chapter 9 gave some suggestions of societies to join, but the following list is more comprehensive.

The British Horse Society*, National Equestrian Centre, Stoneleigh, Kenilworth, Warwicks, C V8 2L R.
The Pony Club* (address as above).
The Association of British Riding Schools*, Old Brewery Yard, Penzance, Cornwall, T R18 2S L.
The Bransby Home of Rest for Horses, Bransby, Saxilby, Lincoln L N1 2P H.
The British Show Hack, Cob and Riding Horse Association*, National Equestrian Centre, Stoneleigh, Kenilworth, Warwicks, C V8 2L R.
British Equestrian Trade Association, Wothersome Grange, Bramham, Wetherby, Yorks, L S23 6L Y.
British Equine Veterinary Association, Park Lodge, Bells Yew Green Road, Frant, Tunbridge Wells, Kent, T N3 9E B.
British Show Jumping Association*, British Equestrian Centre, Kenilworth, Warwicks, C V8 2L R.
The Coaching Club*, 2 Treville Street, Roehampton, London S W15.

Commons, Open Spaces and Footpaths Preservation Society*, 25a Bell Street, Henley-on-Thames, Oxon, R G9 2B A.

Endurance Horse and Pony Society of Great Britain*, 6 Lundy View, Northem, Bideford, Devon.

Equine Behaviour Study Circle*, 9 Rostherne Avenue, Lowton St Lukes, Warrington, Cheshire, W A3 2Q D.

Farriers' Registration Council, 4 Royal College Street, London N W1 0T U.

Hurlingham Polo Association*, Ambersham Farm, Midhurst, West Sussex, G U29 0B X.

Ponies of Britain*, Ascot Racecourse, Ascot, Berks, S L5 7J N.

The Side Saddle Association*, Foxworth, Stitchins Hill, Leigh, Sinton, Hereford and Worcester, W R13 5D J.

Society of Master Saddlers Ltd, 138 Plumstead Common Road, Plumstead, London S E18 2U L.

Western Horsemen's Association of Great Britain*, 65 Weald Bridge Road, North Weald, Essex, C M16 6E S.

British Driving Society*, 27 Duggard Place, Barford, Warwicks, C V35 8D X.

British Hay and Straw Merchants' Association, Hoval House, Orchard Parade, Mutton Lane, Potters Bar, Herts, E N6 3A R.

British Show Pony Society*, 124 Green End Road, Sawtry, Huntingdon, Cambs.

Horses and Ponies Protection Association*, Greenbank Farm, Fence, Burnley, Lancs.

National Pony Society*, 7 Cross and Pillory Lane, Alton, Hants.

Breed Societies

Arab Horse Society*, Goddards Green, Cranbrook, Kent, T N17 3L P.

British Andalusian Horse Society*, Church Farm, Church Street, Semington, Trowbridge, Wilts, B A14 6J S.

British Appaloosa Society*, Ash Cottage, Icombe, Stow-on-the-Wold, Glos.

British Morgan Horse Society*, George and Dragon Hall, Mary Place, London W11.

British Palomino Society*, Llanynis, Builth Wells, Powys, L D2 3H H.

British Quarter Horse Association Ltd*, The Mill House, Lubenham, Market Harborough, Leics, B A2 7E F.

British Warm-blood Society*, 140 Wadacre Lane, Melling, Liverpool, Merseyside, L31 1D2.

Dales Pony Society*, 55 Cromwell Street, Walkley, Sheffield, Yorks, S6 3R N.

Dartmoor Pony Society*, Weston Manor, Corscombe, Dorchester, Dorset, D T2 0P B.

English Connemara Pony Society*, 2 The Leys, Salford, Chipping Norton, Oxon.

Exmoor Pony Society*, Quarry Cottage, Sampford Brett, Williton, Somerset.

Fell Pony Society*, 19 Dragley Beck, Ulverston, Cumbria, L A12 0H D.

Highland Pony Society*, Orwell House, Milnathort, Kinross-shire, K Y13 7Y Q.

Irish Draught Horse Society (GB)*, 4th Street, National Agricultural Centre, Stoneleigh, Warwicks, C V8 2L G.

National Light Horse Breeding Society*, 8 Market Square, Westerham, Kent, T N16 1A W.

New Forest Pony and Cattle Breeding Society*, Beacon Corner, Burley, Ringwood, Hants, B H24 4E W.

Shetland Pony Stud Book Society*, 8 Whinfield Road, Montrose, Angus, D D10 8S A.

Welsh Pony and Cob Society*, 6 Chalybeate Street, Aberystwyth, Dyfed, S Y23 1H S.

Other useful names and addresses

Equine Management Consultancy Service, The Small Hall, The Old School, Shrivenham Road, Highworth, Wilts, S N6 7B Z. (Scientifically based yet practical advice on all aspects of equine management. Quick advice service. Weight- and height-measuring tapes for sale.)

Equi-Study Ltd, Hole House, Haltwhistle, N E49 0L Q. (Correspondence courses in horsemastership.)

FarmKey Ltd, Banbury, Oxon. (Freeze-marking security service and register for animals, also tack security scheme.)

J.A. Allen Ltd, 1 Lower Grosvenor Place, off Buckingham Palace Road, London S W1 0E L. (New, used, out-of-print and antiquarian books.)

Spetech Ltd, Grey Mead Lodge, Thame Park Road, Thame O X9 3PL ('Unbustable' buckets etc.)

Appendix B
Recommended Books

Horse and Stable Management, J. Houghton Brown and V. Powell-Smith, Granada Publishing, 1984.
Safety With Horses, B. Giles, Stanley Paul, 1985.
The Urban Horseman, S. Gordon, Longman, 1983.
Horse Tack, J. Richardson, Pelham Books, 1982.
The Horse's Mind, L. Rees, Stanley Paul, 1984.
Keeping a Horse Outdoors, S. McBane, David & Charles, 1984.
Horse Ailments and Health Care, C. Vogel B VetMed., M R C V S, Ward Lock, 1982.
Inside the Horse, P.D. Rossdale, M A, F R C V S, California Thoroughbred Breeders Association, 1976. Available from J.A. Allen Ltd (see Appendix A).
A Guide to Driving Horses, S. Walrond, Pelham Books, 1971 and 1977.
The Horse, Structure and Movement, R.H. Smythe, M R C V S, revised by P.C. Goody, BSc, PhD, Allen, 1972.
Farriery, J. Hickman, M A, F R C V S, Allen, 1977.
Reflections on the Art of Horsemanship, H.J. Heyer, Allen, 1968.
Riding Side-Saddle, J. Macdonald and V. Francis, Pelham.
The Horse's Health from A–Z, P.D. Rossdale and S.M. Wreford, David & Charles, 1974.
Horse Anatomy, P.C. Goody, BSc, PhD, J.A. Allen Ltd.

In addition to the titles listed above, the British Horse Society publishes a wide range of books on various aspects of horse management and riding.